Trolleybuses- Glasgow's Silent Service
Hugh Dougherty

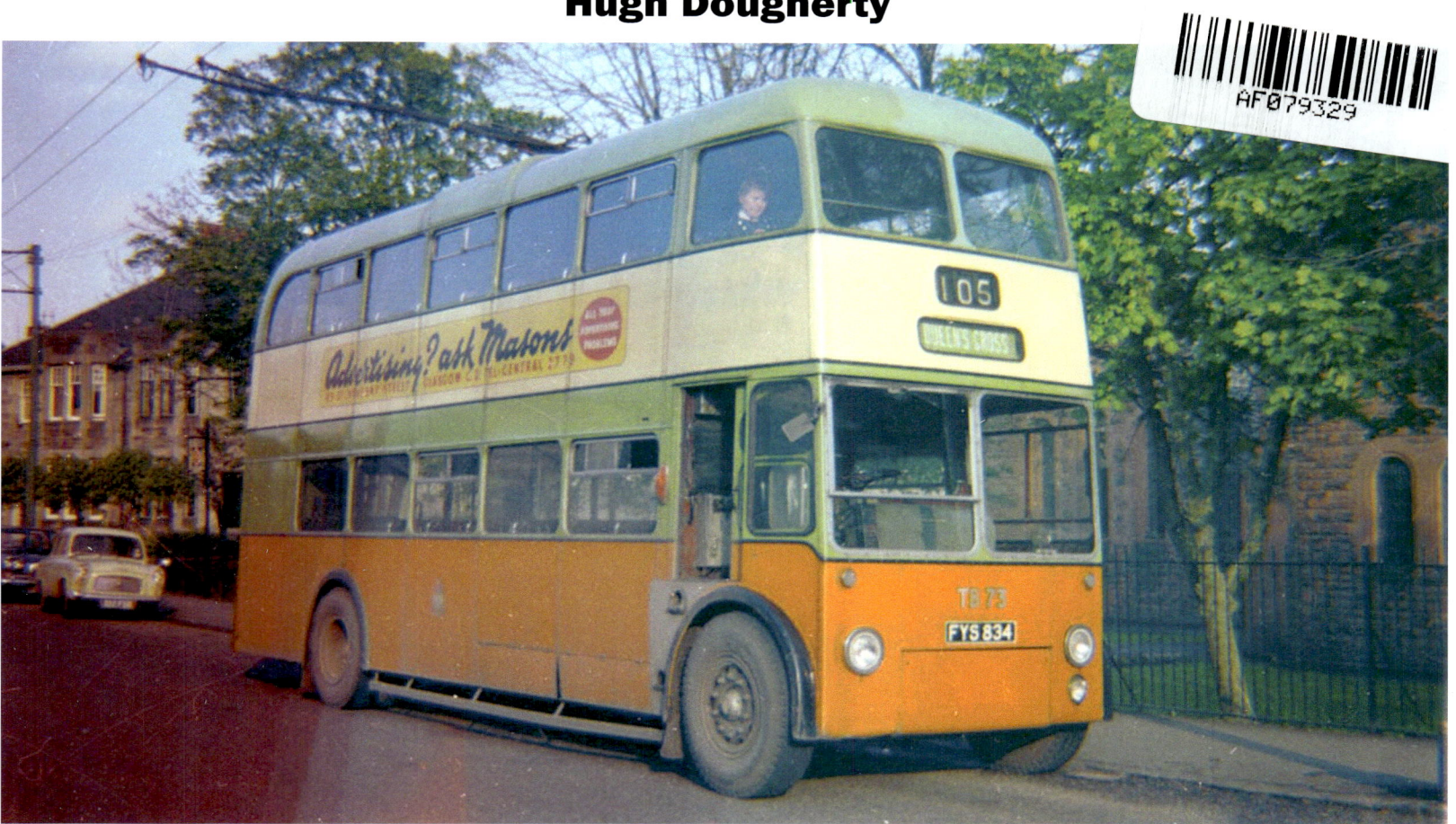

The 105 reached well-to-do Clarkston in Renfrewshire. On 25th May 1967, TB73 waits its time to depart for Queen's Cross, while its clippie enjoys a read on the top deck. There was no secret about the Masons mentioned on the side panel of the bus. It was an advertising agency! *Hugh Dougherty*

© Hugh Dougherty, 2024
First published in the United Kingdom, 2024,
by Stenlake Publishing Ltd.
www.stenlake.co.uk
ISBN 978-1-84033-982-6

The publishers regret that they cannot supply
copies of any pictures featured in this book.

Printed by
P2D Books, 1 Newlands Rd, Westoning, Bedford, MK45 5LD

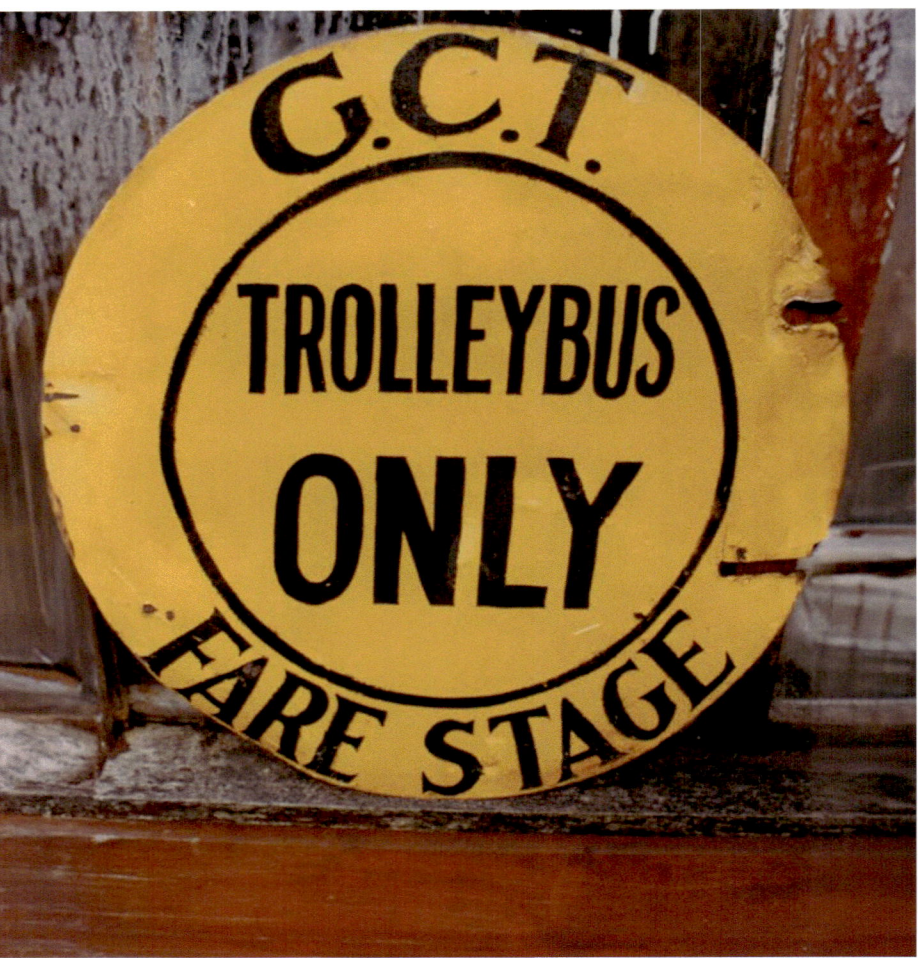

Trolleybus fare stage sign. *Hugh Dougherty*

Discovering the Glasgow Trolleybus

I was a wee boy of three when I first discovered the wonder that was the Glasgow trolleybus in 1953. We lived in Lochleven Road, up a 'wally' (tiled) close, with white, pipe-clayed stairs. And, although our main drag, Battlefield Road, echoed daily to the rising and falling hum of tram motors, as their motormen notched up their controllers, and the metallic ring and clatter of tram wheels on the points outside Battlefield Rest, we didn't have any trolleybuses. We even had Langside Depot at the end of the road, and, within its dark interior, there were trams, trams and more trams, and not a trolleybus in sight.

But I did come across the trolleys and was left with a lasting impression of my first 'hurl' on one of these orange, cream and green silent vehicles, when my mother took me to visit Dr Colvin, our family doctor, whose surgery was down in the Gorbals on Crown Street, reached by trolleybus from Mount Florida.

Up at the Mount, the twin, trolleybus wires shared space with the trams on route 12. That was the tram that took us to Mass at Holy Cross Church on Sunday mornings, as we waited at the end of our street on Battlefield Road to spot a 12 coming out of the depot, to go on service at Mount Florida terminus.

Although the crews shouldn't have, as the tram didn't enterservice until Mount Florida terminus, they got to look out for us and stopped to pick us up. Off we went on a fascinating trip, doubly, so as it was normally forbidden to ordinary passengers, with the driver changing the points with his heavy points iron, to allow us to take the single track up Prospecthill Road, where, on the sharp curve, the rails, which were laid asphalt, rather than granite setts, would seem to appear from underneath the tram, before we turned left into Cathcart Road. It didn't escape my attention that we had to negotiate crossing the trolleybus wires, accompanied by much, deft, controller handle swinging by the driver, to put the power on and off through the dead sections, and, if it was a dull, winter's morning, there would be impressive sparks, too, as our tram's bow collector found its way through the net of wires above.

Then, using the points iron again, the driver, dressed in his long, green, motorman's coat, and sporting Glasgow Corporation Transport issue tram driver's gloves, turned us back, and ran up to Clincart Road terminus, where there was yet more points changing and the seat backs to swung over, allowing our tram to take up service, and head for Paisley Road Toll.

The clippie would know my Dad, as he travelled on a 12 rush hour, shipyard workers' special each weekday, sitting stolidly, his coat and green, felt hat out of place among the fat capped shipyard workers, but, like them, his piece (Glaswegian for as packed lunch) was wrapped in a Milanda bread wrapper, as he shoogled down to St Gerard's in Govan where he taught. And, if, as was often the case, the conductress was from Donegal, she and my Dad would chat away in Irish, so free Mass transit was guaranteed for family Dougherty!

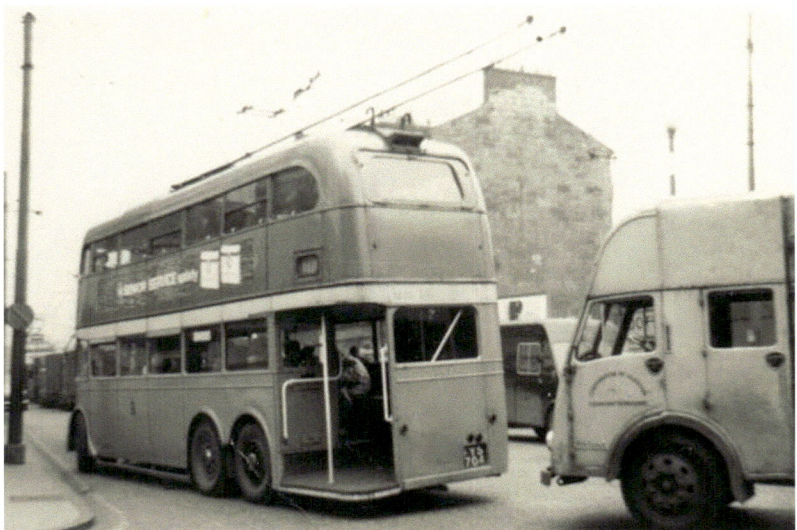

In the Gorbals on Crown Street on 29th April 1966, TB4, near Dr Colvin's surgery, one of the original British United Traction (BUT) trolleybuses of 1949 turns from Rutherglen Road, pursued by a Corporation bin lorry. The 101 and 102 routes were withdrawn the next day and this once busy junction has been obliterated by redevelopment.   *Hugh Dougherty*

Then, there was Hughie the tram driver, an elderly and kindly motorman, who allowed me to sit in his cab, one day, when I was six, at Langside terminus, as he explained to me and my mother how the controls worked. That was when I knew I wanted to be a motorman! Clearly, trolleybuses had a lot to live up to, compared with the trams, but they did offer travel to exotic places, even beyond Holy Cross Church, where the 12 dropped us, and I was up for that.

We went to Dr Colvin as Catholic GPs were hard to find in those days, and who knows what non-Catholic ones might have prescribed (!). In any case, the good doctor's father was quite famous. Also a doctor, he had been involved in defeating an outbreak of plague in Glasgow in 1900, but, best of all, as far as I was concerned, you had to go to and from his surgery by trolleybus. That was a tonic in itself for wee me in those days when no wean's mammy left a surgery without a prescription for some sugar-seething, yellow-tinted tonic with a name like Minadex.

Trolleybuses, Dr Colvin's ground floor tenement consulting rooms, dark Gorbals streets with soot-blackened, sandstone buildings, gas street lights and prescribed, Minadex tonic, with bottles whose corks would never go back in fully, because of encrusted sugar crystals, are entwined in my early memories.

I remember that the trolleys passed almost silently, but with a vague, and not unpleasant, almost hollow 'hum', coming mysteriously from their back bogies, for these were six-wheel buses, Glasgow's original trolleybuses of 1949, and they were quiet beyond belief compared to the Glasgow trams and diesel buses of the day.

That was, in fact, why Glaswegians dubbed them 'Silent Death', the story being that you wouldn't hear them coming, and most homes on the south side, where they ran, would tell you, perhaps years later, about their relative who was mown down by a trolley. "Uncle Seamus bought it in Allison Street under a 108," your plumber would tell you. "He never heard the trolleybus coming. They sneaked up on you and were silent death."

And 'silent death' did hit the international headlines when, on 9th November 1964, USA singing star, Dionne Warwick, exiting after an appearance, from the stage door of the Odeon Cinema on to West Nile Street, was knocked down by a trolleybus, which, the press reported, loomed silently out of the fog before hitting her.

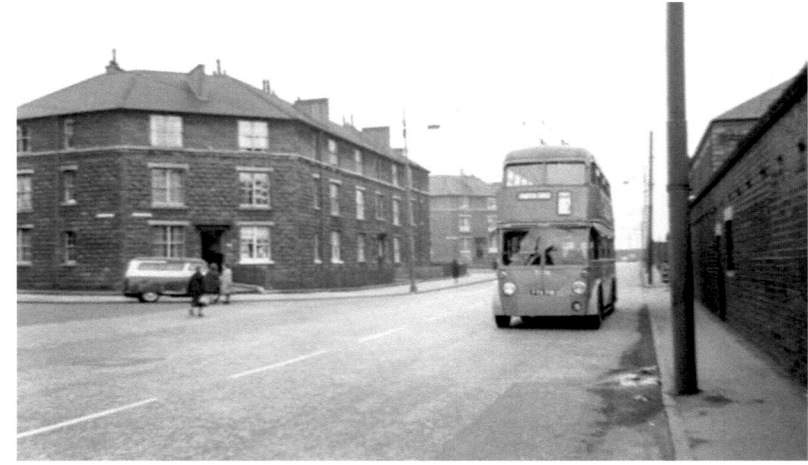

TB18 shows a clean pair of heels on its way to Hampden Garage at shift's end in February 1966 on Aikenhead Road, passing then-unrefurbished 1930s tenements on the left and the former North British Locomotive Company Queen's Park Works on the right. *Hugh Dougherty*

Dionne, who joked after the incident, that she hadn't managed to 'Walk on By', was treated in hospital for minor injuries, and the driver became a celebrity in Hampden Garage.

Many Glaswegians said that it proved that trolleybuses did live up to their nickname. Strange that, today, much is made of battery-electric buses, being silent, but the reason for the trolleys being dubbed 'silent death', lay in the fact that the trams they replaced were noisy, as were the city's diesel buses. You could hear both coming a mile away, and, when the diesels were put on the streets, the transport department ran campaigns to stop passengers walking out into the middle of the road, which they'd been used to doing, to board their trams.

For many years, there was a superb mural on the rear, inside wall of Battlefield Rest, showing a 1930s motorbus, and a lady standing at a stop, to remind passengers to always signal from the kerb, and to stay there until the bus pulled in. The warning applied equally to trolleybuses, which, thanks to being able to move under their wires, also picked up from the kerb.

But, to me, as a three year old, I loved the silence of the trolleys, and a visit to Dr Colvin, was to be savoured. We would sit downstairs, on the very comfortable, green, moquette seats, just behind the nearside bulkhead of the driver's cab. That gave you a clear view ahead, as we swept through Govanhill, with the trolley showing a fair turn of speed.

Once, the clippie advised my mother to keep me sitting on the seat, rather than standing on her knee for a better view, as the bulkhead window could be opened and I might end up in the cab. "Ye, see, hen," as my mother would recall the clippie solemnly telling her, "yon cab's full of electricity, so it is, an' yer wean could get electrified!"

I never did get electrocuted by a trolley, nor did one steal up on me, to live up to its nickname, and as I grew, I realised that the city's superb trams, which had disappeared from our Battlefield Road in 1957, and which were scrapped entirely in 1962, were being cruelly butchered on the altar of the Great God Car.

The trolleybus, in essence, a trackless tram, was its worthy successor, keeping alive Glasgow's best traditions of electric street traction, declaring its very presence through its clearly-visible overhead wires.

There was a lot to learn about the trolleys, and, during my teenage years I made sure that I found out all I could about them, up until their reign was cut short, both cruelly and prematurely, on 27th May 1967, when Silent Death itself died. That was long before anyone considered the environment, and when the particulates from the polluting replacement diesel buses, were studiously ignored. It was held that they could get out of the way of the all-conquering car more effectively than the wire-tied trolleys.

Glasgow, despite having one of the lowest rates of car ownership in Britain at the time, nailed its colours firmly to the mast of motoring and motorways, buoyed up by the Government-commissioned Buchanan Report of 1963, which said that there would be cars, cars and more cars in cities and that they should be altered to accommodate them. Fixed transport systems, such as trams and trolleybuses, simply got in the way of cars, and diesel buses should be used to cater for the few unfortunates without their own wheels. No wonder the trolleybuses bit the dust, just five years after the last tram ran in 1962, and when the trolleybus fleet, hardly ten years old, was sold at a massive loss for scrap. What mistakes were made in the 1960s, and what a lasting effect they have had ever since.

This short book records my impressions of the Glasgow trolleybuses as a youngster and, as we struggle with battery buses, vague talk of a Glasgow Metro, and continuing traffic congestion, I believe that the trolleybus, like the Glasgow tram, should never have been scrapped. Had trolleybuses been retained and developed, they would now be playing a key role in an environmentally-friendly and efficient public transport service, wooing passengers away from their cars, and providing Glasgow with the decent transport service it so desperately needs and certainly deserves.

Join me on my journey back to the days of Glasgow's silent service. Sit back, enjoy the ride and celebrate that silence!

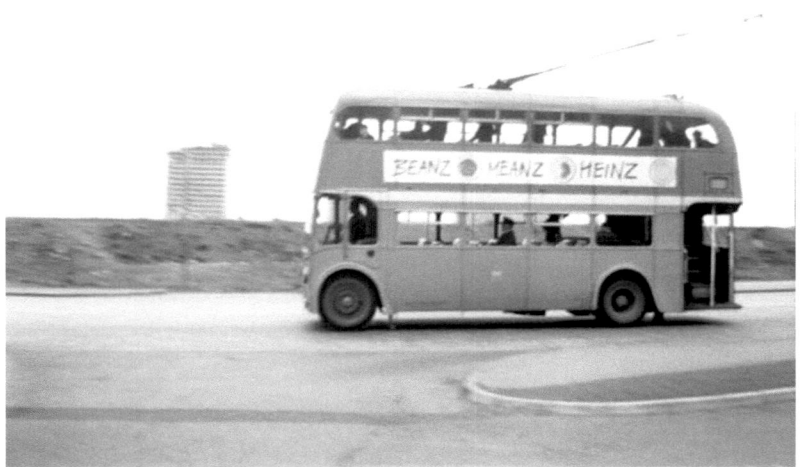

Beanz Means Speed for this four-wheeler Sunbeam, accelerating away from a stop on Aikenhead Road, as passengers fight the g-forces to get to their seats in February 1966. The now-demolished multi-storey Toryglen Circus high flats are being built in the background. *Hugh Dougherty*

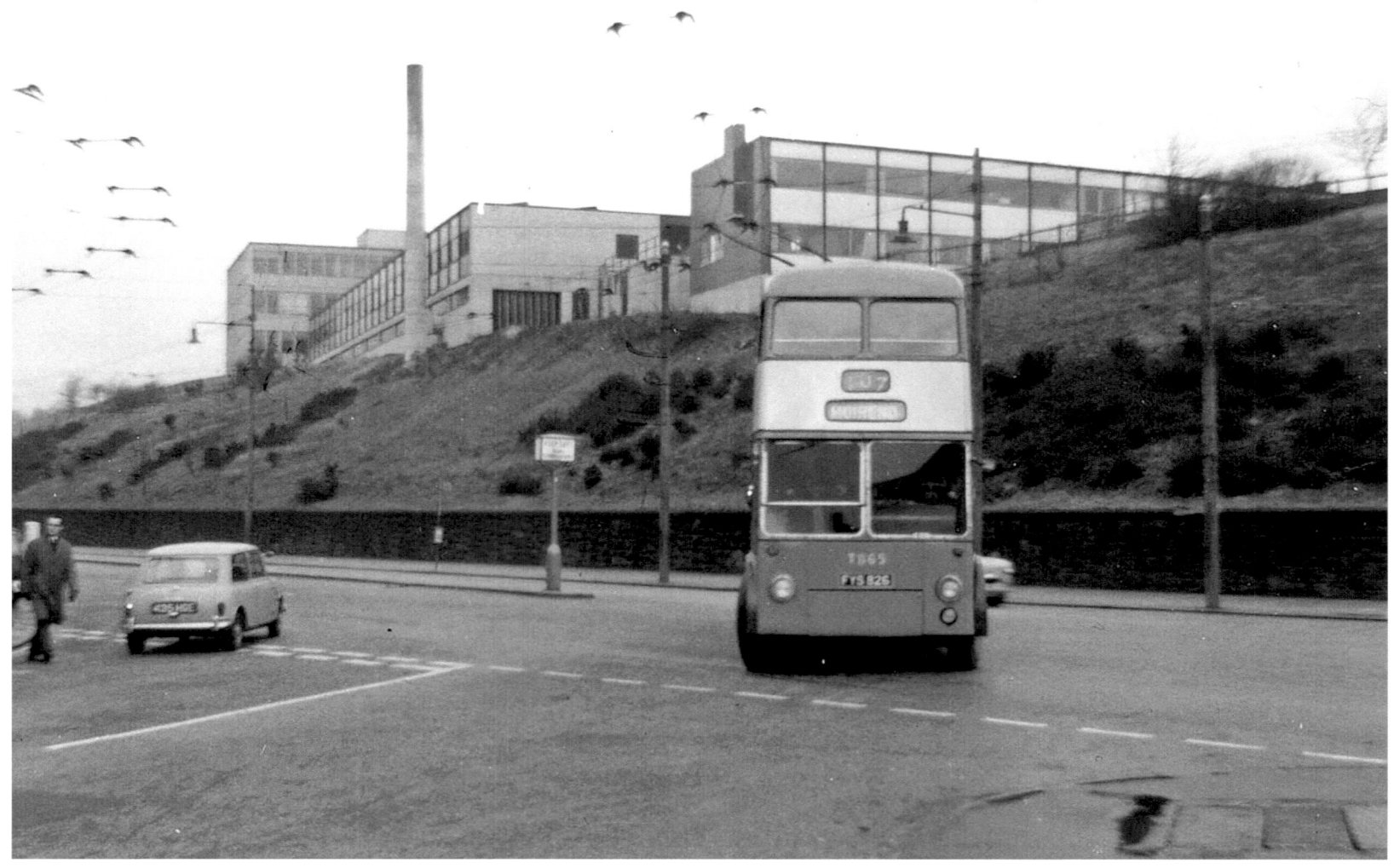

The 107s ran along our Battlefield Road from 1957 onwards. TB65, new that year, turns into Holmlea Road on its way to Muirend on 28th January 1967, with the then-new Langside College extension behind.

Hugh Dougherty

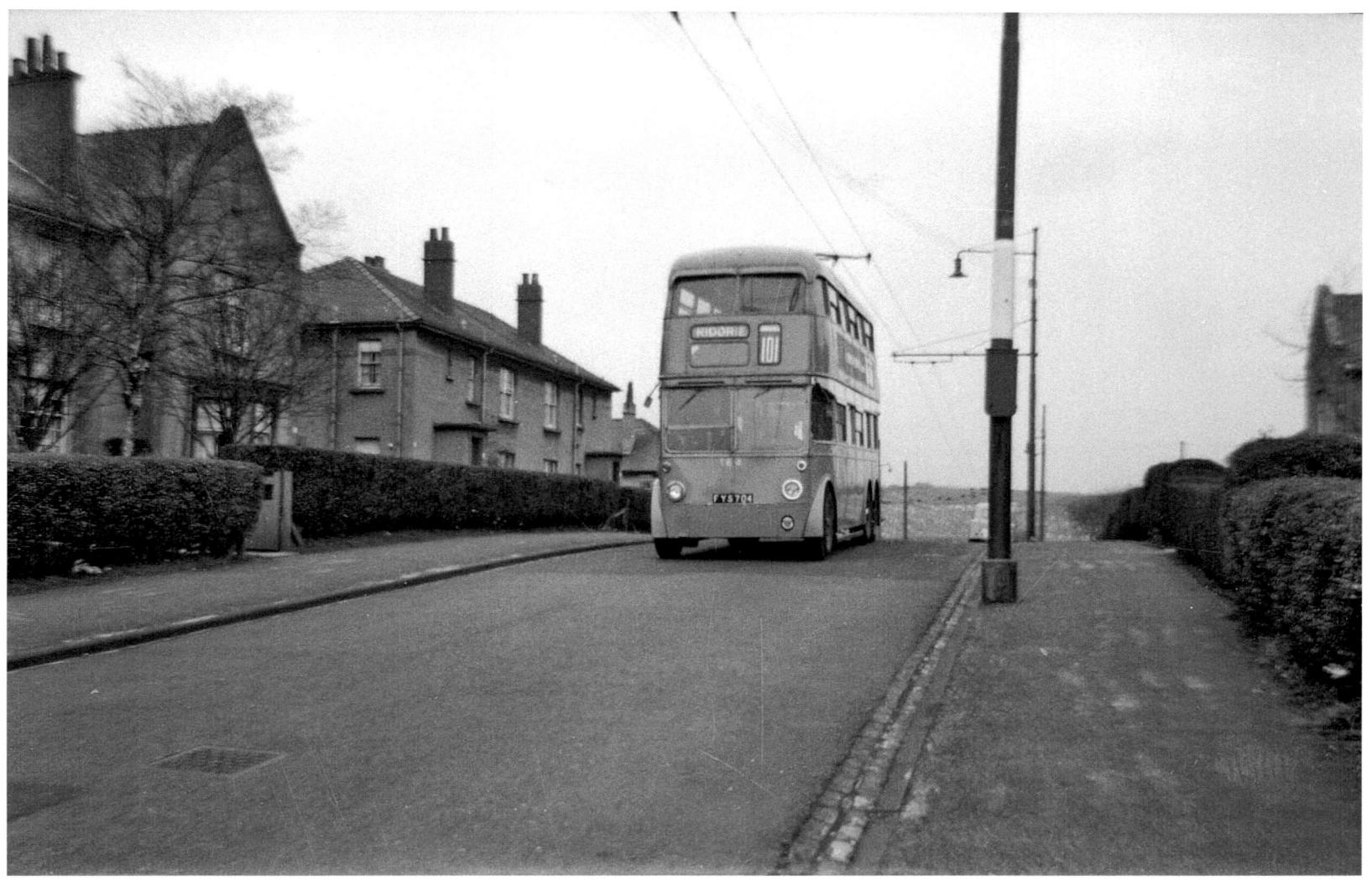

At the northern extremity of route 101, TB4 runs round the turning circle at Riddrie, the white band on the pole telling the driver to take his foot off the accelerator at the section feeder on the overhead line, on 29th April 1966. *Hugh Dougherty.*

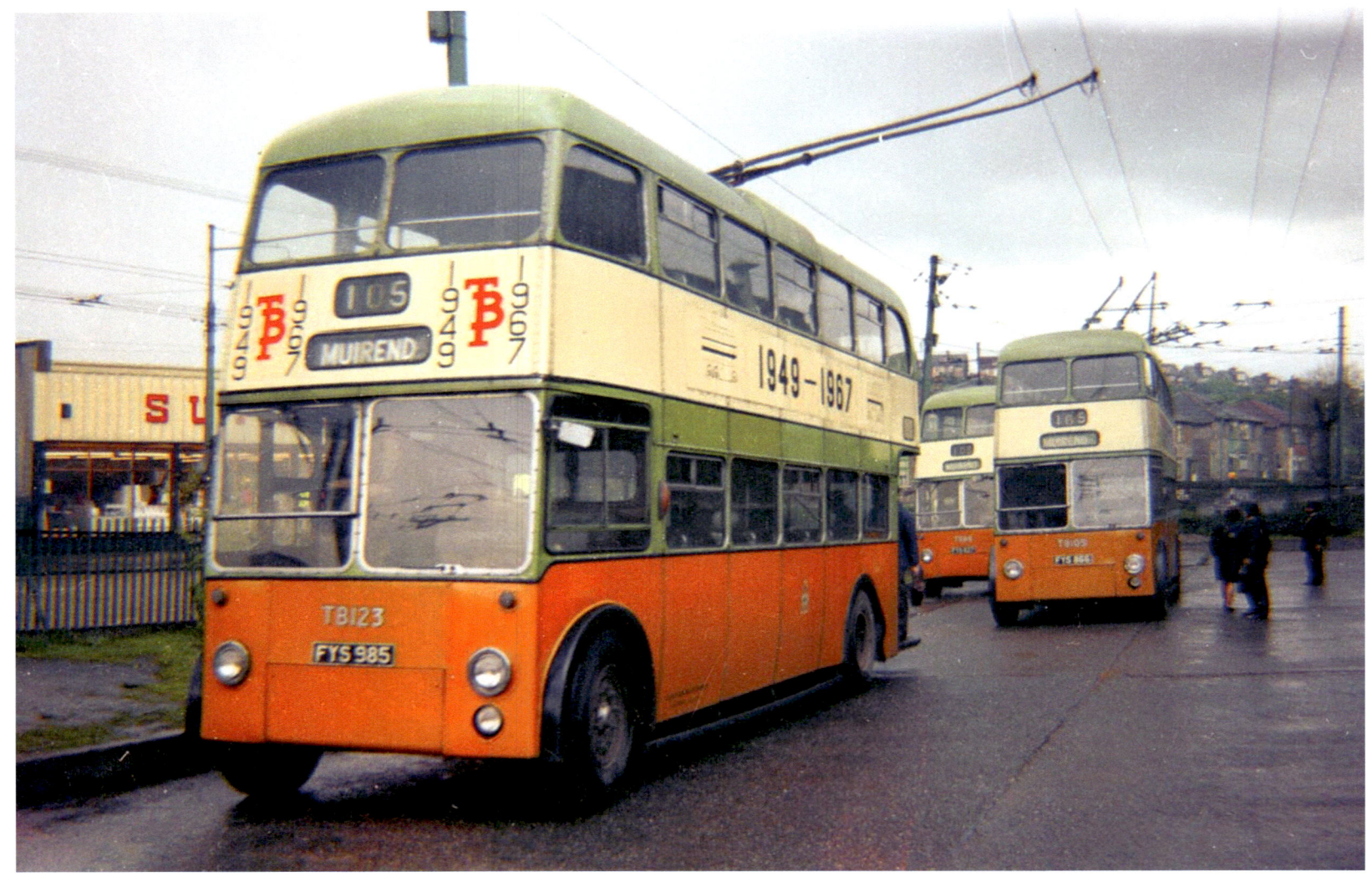

On 25th May 1967, two days before the end of the trolleybuses, TB123, the final trolley built for Glasgow, carrying its Last Trolleybus Week posters, leaves the Hampden Garage forecourt, with TBs 105 and 66 on rush hour specials.

Hugh Dougherty

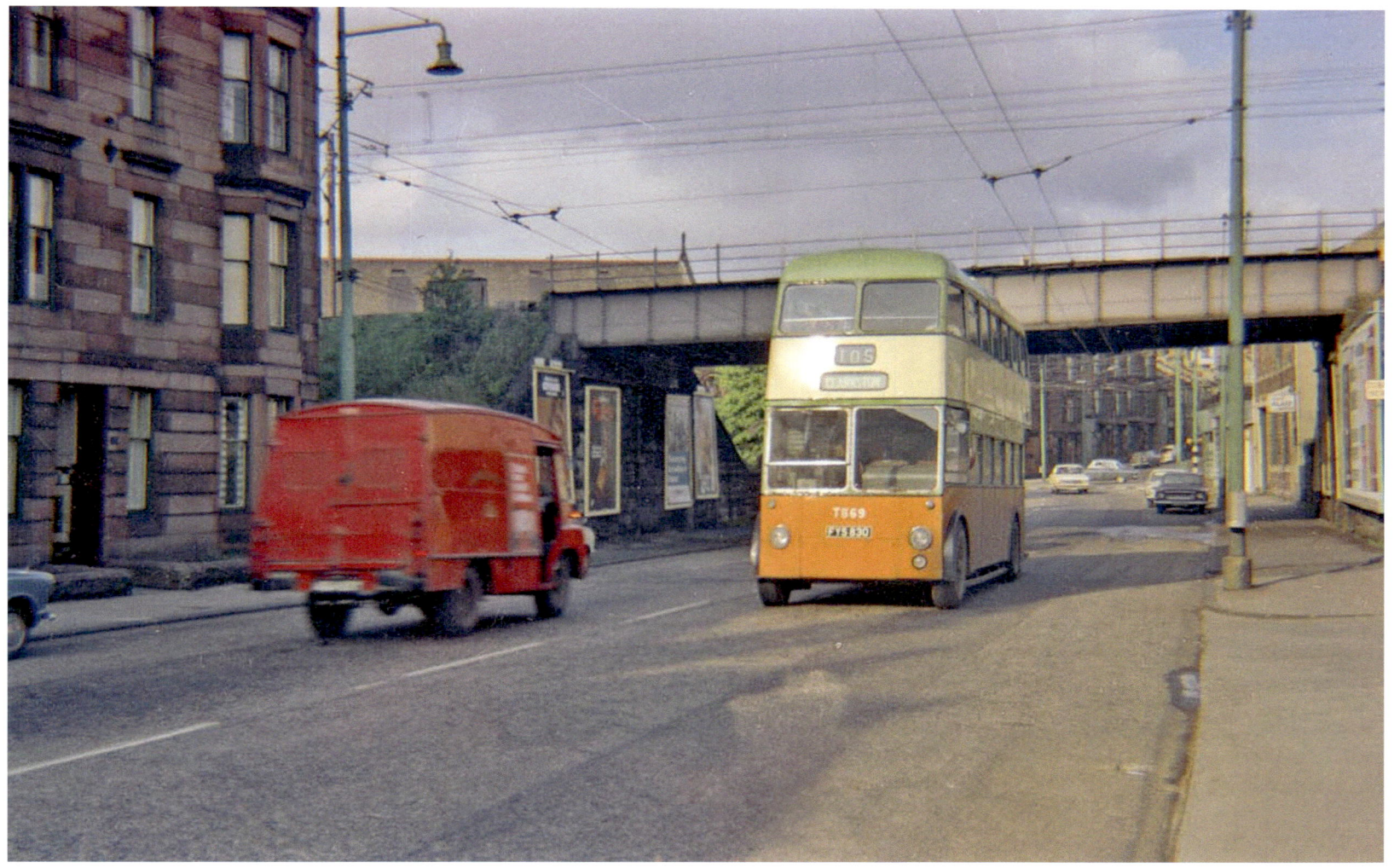

TB69 comes out from under the Cathcart Circle railway bridge on the sunny evening of 25th May 1967. As this was the day on which Celtic won the European Cup, the streets were very quiet! One Hampden driver who finished his shift and left for Lisbon, still in his green uniform, was feted by locals there as they thought he was a very specially-dressed Celtic fan!

Hugh Dougherty

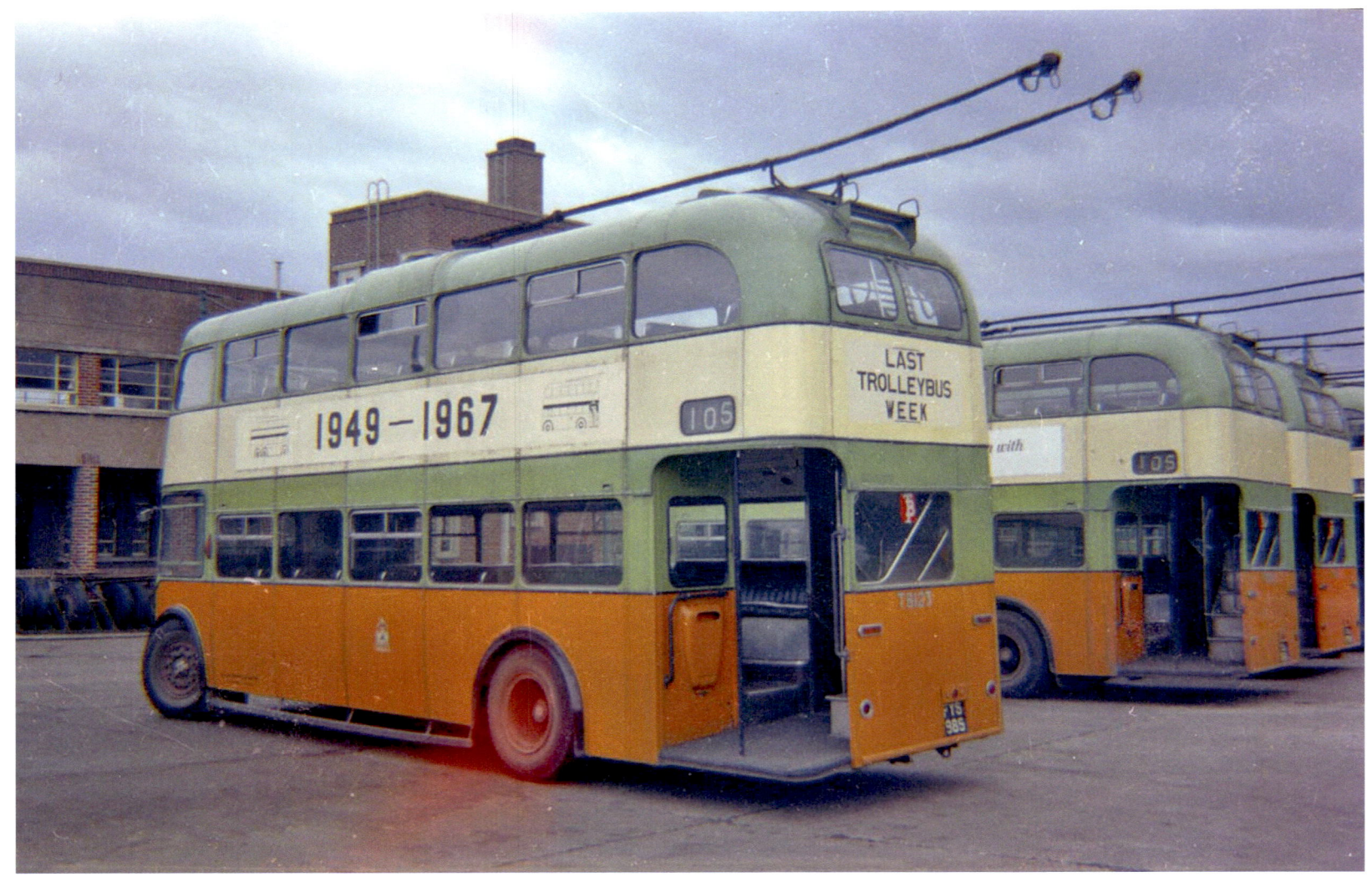

Lined up in Hampden Garage on 25th May 1967, with just two days of life left, are TB123 and other trolleys. It was astonishing that these trolleys, built just nine years earlier, were sold for scrap.

Hugh Dougherty

By Trolleybus to School

In November 1957, just before our number 5 tram, linking the south side and west end, via, then, swish, Sauchiehall Street, was replaced by the 43 bus, two sets of trolleybus wires appeared alongside the tramway overhead on Battlefield Road. I found this quite intriguing, and, in due course, I spotted trolleybuses running under the wires on newly-established route 107. They hummed along Battlefield Road on their way to Maitland Street, 'up the town,' as true south siders describe a trip to the city centre, and south, to Muirend.

I was captivated by these new trolleys, more modern than the six wheelers that took us to Dr Colvin's in Gorbals. Even as a six year-old, I did notice that they had four wheels only, and were painted in the same orange colour as the trams wore below their lower deck windows. There had to be a connection, and, best of all, sparks came from their trolleyheads as they passed under some sections of wires- just like the trams we'd lost. These were worthy successors to our late, lamented 5 trams.

Fast forward to Tuesday 4th September 1962, and, an 11 year-old boy stood with his mother, just after teatime, on the crowded pavement, at the end of Albert Drive, in pouring rain, to mourn the last Glasgow trams making their way into Coplawhill Car Works. He was there, along with the rest of Glasgow, or, at least, the estimated quarter-of-a-million people who lined the route from Dalmarnock Depot, most unconvinced that scrapping the trams was wise.

That 11 year-old was me, and, soaked and dejected, after the last tram had disappeared into Coplawhill forever, when Glasgow lost so much of its character, self-assurance and certainty that comes from having a tram system, we walked up to Victoria Road, to catch a trusty 107. Definitely, I told myself, a trackless tram, and the next best thing. Our trolley was crammed with other last tram mourners returning from the funeral. "Ah'm an auld tramway man masel," the conductor announced to the bus, which was full on both decks. "So youse can all have a free hurl hame!"

I had started in first year at St Aloysius' College in Garnethill, then a grant-aided school with token fees, and, although run by the Jesuits, still then, very much an integral part of Glasgow

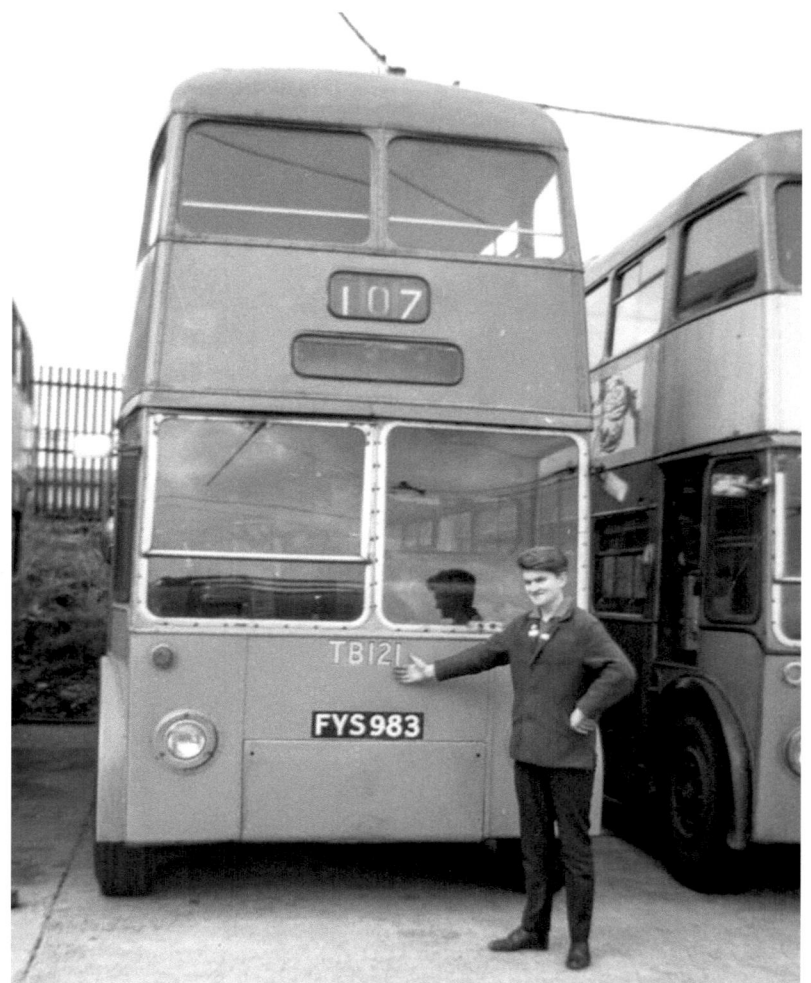

A 16-year-old Hugh, who should have been studying for his Highers (!) stands beside TB121, his regular trolley home from school, as it awaits its fate at Hampden, following the withdrawal of the 107 route in March 1967.
Paul Adams

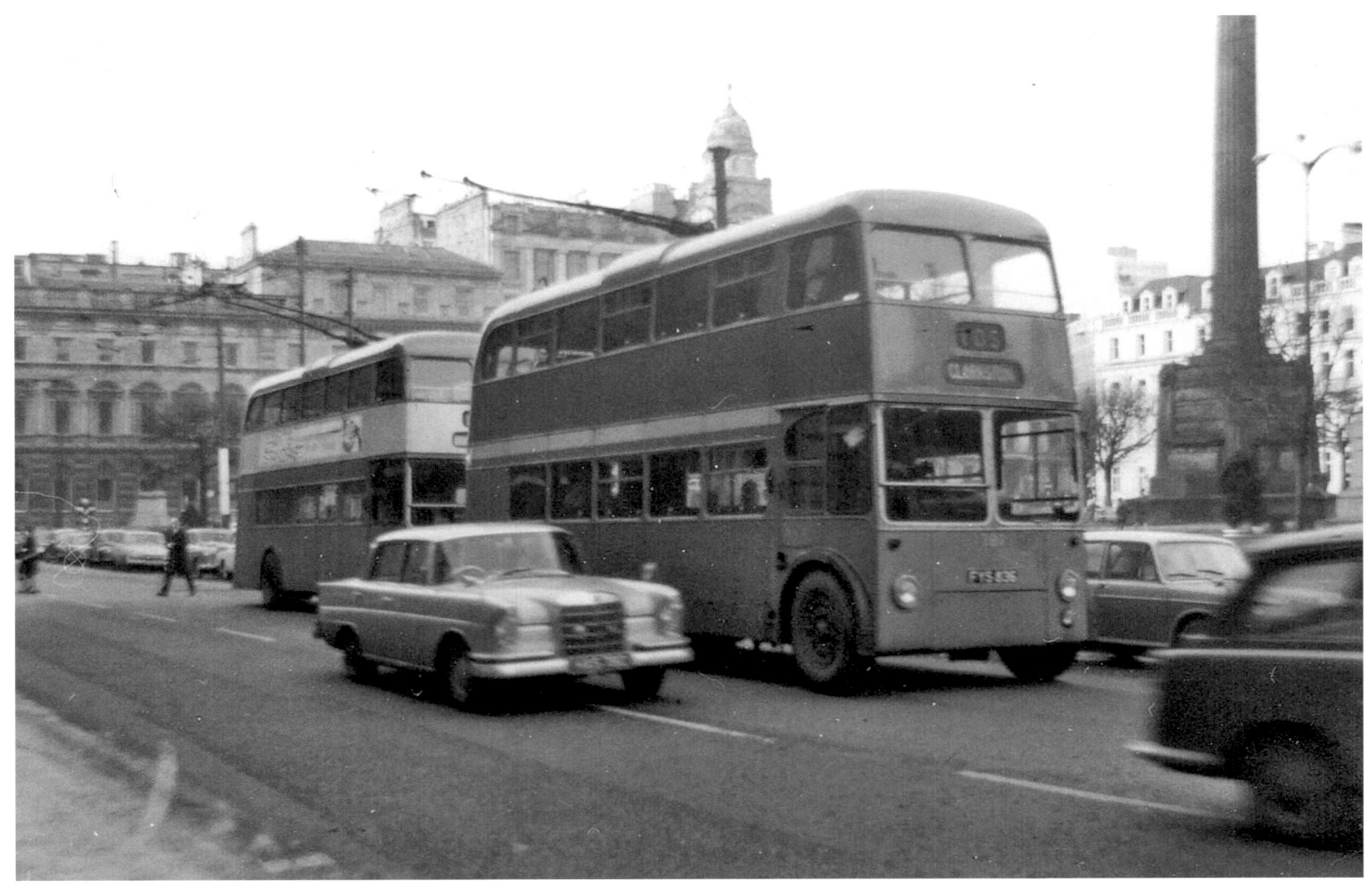

Hugh's trolley to school took him through the heart of Glasgow at George Square where TB75 on the 105 leads a 107 for Clarkston and Muirend on a dull Saturday, 4th February 1967.

Hugh Dougherty

Corporation Education Department, a world away from today's expensive and elite, independent institution.

I had to decide how best to get there, and, as a trolleybus fan, I have to confess, initially took the then-new Blue Trains, which had been introduced in May 1962, on our local Cathcart Circle line. These were fast, efficient and modern, and whisked me from Mount Florida Station into Central for the walk up the town to Garnethill.

There was the added attraction that Gus, the 15-year-old boy porter at Mount Florida Station, was a bit of a pal, and I would linger at the station after I got off the train from school, to talk trains with Gus, and to play snap with the collected, expired season tickets. The fact that he wore Rangers socks and I wore a green uniform, didn't seem to come into it at all!

But Gus moved on to a higher calling in Central Station, and my thoughts turned to the 107 to Maitland Street, and took the 107 from then on in. I would board at the same stop that had been there from the dawn of tramway time, and, in those days, most local people, travelling to their offices in town, would take the trolley or the 5 or 14 diesel buses. You just turned up and there was a trolleybus or bus every couple of minutes at a frequency level that no one would recognise today.

For me, it had to be the trolley, and, I would walk to the stop, wearing my uniform, school case crammed full of homework from the night before, for the 8.5 am 107 to Maitland Street terminus. I would be joined in the queue by the respectability of Battlefield, men in suits, and even one or two in bowler hats, with briefcase and umbrella on wet days, and no-nonsense business ladies. The older ones dressed in severe 'costumes' of grey skirt and top, with stern faces to match. You wouldn't have messed with them, and manners dictated that you stood back to allow them to gain the platform, before you.

Several queue members would be smoking, of course. This was a time when men with pipes were a common sight, and, as the 107 arrived in a hiss of air brakes at the stop, drawing into the kerb, with its trolleys, magically and obediently following the overhead wires above the vehicle's trajectory, the queue would split into the inside and upstairs persuasions. Smokers, of course went aloft, to glory in the fug that stained the white paintwork of the upper deck inside roofs, yellow rendering the 'No Spitting" sign nearly illegible.

My trolley usually came at 8.05, as my carefully kept records of those days tell me now, but, if you missed that, the next one was just three minutes behind, so there was no need to worry, unlike the city gent, all red face and bristling moustache, who was denied entry one morning by the south Asian conductor, as the bus was full.

"Sorry, full up!" the conductor intoned as he held out his outstretched hand to repel boarders, to which the gent replied: "You black b------!" Coolly, the conductor stretched across to the platform bell push, belled the bus away, and as it swished off with the initial burst of speed that all the trolleys exhibited, exclaimed: "You white b-----!" And he and his bus were gone.

The man was furious, but all of us in the queue sniggered at his expense. The conductor had conducted himself more than well. Maybe race relations issues were dealt with more directly and effectively in those days…..

Once on board, I headed upstairs, bracing myself for the g-force that pushed you backwards on a trolleybus as the drivers notched up, the whine of the motor rising with the speed, and made for the inside seat on the driver's side, one back from the front. There, you could open the window to let some of the smoke out, although the same man who got on every morning at Battlefield Rest, and sat beside me, would tut and smoke his fag ever more furiously. Practically every passenger read a newspaper avidly. It was still the age of newsprint.

It's a world that's hard to recall, as is also the fact that there were no heaters on the trolleybuses. On really cold mornings, as the buses sat out overnight at Hampden Garage, the inside of the windows were iced up. If I worked hard I could usually scrape off enough to see out by George Square, for people had different thermostats and concepts of comfort then, and no one felt that a freezing trolley was unacceptable.

The crews, of course, worked on an unheated trolley all shift, although Glasgow Corporation did eventually give in to union pressure and a small, electric heater was attached to the steering columns of the later-built trolleys, to keep drivers from seizing up with hypothermia. That was the only concession to the green

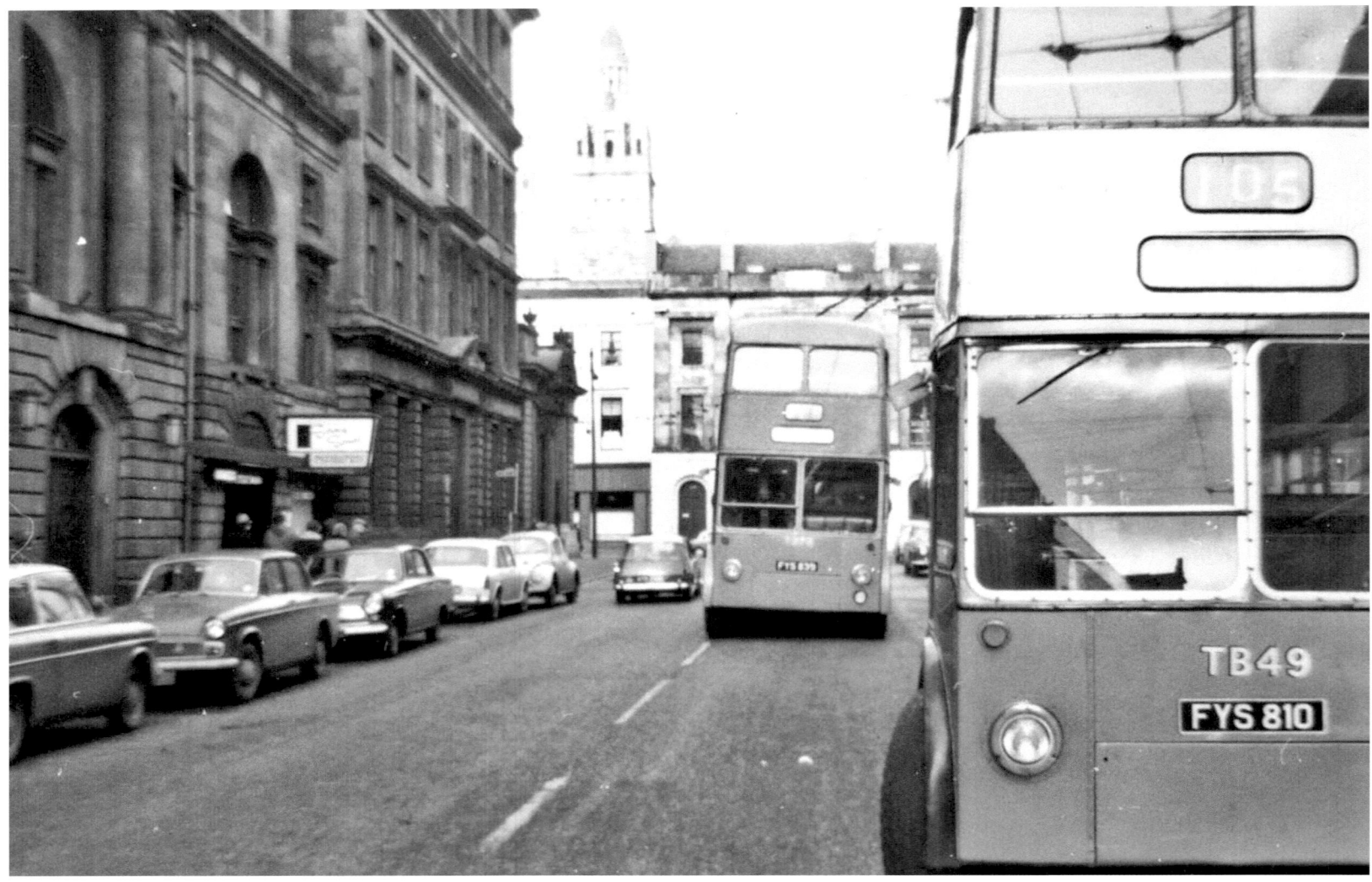

TB49, broken down with a flat tyre, and trolleys off the wires, awaits rescue, while TB78 passes the Glasgow Trades House on Glassford Street on Saturday 4th February 1967.

Hugh Dougherty

staff's comfort, and, in summer, they sweltered in their regulation uniforms, although, unlike on diesel buses, the driver didn't have engine heat to contend with.

What is remarkable is just how quickly the trolleybus took me to school daily. My wee green book in which I kept my trolleybus records, looked just like a GCT official document thanks to its cover. I bought it from the wee priest who kept the school stock cupboard. He taught French with gusto, and known as "Wee Bella", aka Father Greenwood, you took your filled jotter to him for inspection, before he granted a replacement. He sold his 6d each, green notebooks to keen French pupils to list vocabulary and idioms, and assumed that mine was for the same worthy purpose. He never suspected that it would be filled with the language of the trolleybus, instead of reflexive verbs!

That wee green book, now a historical document itself opens a door into a past world. I kept it after the last trolleybus in 1967, and it shows that I meticulously recorded every trolleybus journey- what a typical thing for a schoolboy of the period to do! It shows, for example, that on the last day of February in 1967, I caught TB100 at 8.6am, passed Eglinton Toll at 8.12, Gorbals Cross at 8.15, Trongate at 8.19, George Square at 8.21 and got off at Maitland Street at 8.25.

The short journey time was down to fewer private cars on the road than now, fast and efficient trolley running, and very short dwell times at stops, thanks to conductors taking fares after people had boarded and were seated, avoiding today's time-consuming queues around the entrances of driver-only buses. You simply could not cover the same journey by bus, currently, in just 19 minutes, with around 40 being more realistic, so far have we advanced over the last 60 or so years…..

I'd record the passing trolleybuses instead of swotting up on my Latin verbs, as well as incidents and breakdowns, and a couple do stand out, such as our conductor being left behind at the Bundy clock outside the nurses' home on Grange Road.

Bundy clocks, named after their inventor, Willard Le Grand Bundy, were strategically placed around the Glasgow tram, trolleybus and bus system, to ensure that services ran to time. Housed in green-painted kerbside cabinets, each with a clock face, time slot and lever, the Bundies required the conductor or clippie to use the time card that he or she carried, usually stuffed into their uniform tunic. The card was inserted into the time slot and a lever pulled to record the vehicle's passing time at the Bundy. There were dire penalties for running early and the time cards would be examined at the end of the shift for infringements.

On the morning in question, our conductor got off for the Bundy as passengers were boarding, put in the card, and a successful recording producing a loud 'ding'. Hearing this, our driver decided that he'd heard the bus bell, rather than the Bundy's, and notched up, leaving the conductor, complete with time card, ticket machine and cash bag standing on the pavement. Some clever passenger, sitting on the back seat, belled the trolley all the way into town, and nearly everyone enjoyed a free ride!

Again, at the same spot, the clippie, too intent on stamping her Bundy card, let far too many passengers board, a mortal sin in the Glasgow Corporation Transport list of offences contained in the trolleybus section rule book, and, as the driver applied power on the slight upwards gradient, the main switch on the platform canopy blew out with an impressive bang. The trolleybus, now powerless, dribbled to a halt and all I could hear from my upstairs perch was some impressive swearing from the cab and a clear shout of "gie the switch a chug, hen!"

This the clippie did, and the breaker blew again under the still excessive load. I vividly recall the sound of the sliding cab door crashing open, watching the driver clambering down from his cab and mayhem ensuing on the rear platform as he threw off enough passengers to make sure that no more than the regulation five standees were on board. When I got off at Maitland Street terminus, the driver and clippie were having a stand-up row using language also banned by the rule book.

Most journeys as my wee, green book shows, went without a hitch, for a well-driven trolleybus, running on roads which were kept in a far superior condition to today's cratered, city arteries in Glasgow, was a joy to travel on. The buses were swift, mostly silent, the only noises being a slight hum from the motor, the occasional buzz from the dewirement indicator when the trolleyheads passed under a dead section in the overhead wires, the whirr of the air compressor cutting in when brake air pressure dropped, the ting of the conductor's bell, the click of the Ultimate ticket machine and a slight drumming on the upper deck roof from the trolleys as they picked their way under the overhead wires and negotiated overhead wire junctions and crossings.

But, I did record one spectacular incident. The 107s shared wires with 105s between Gorbals and Cowcaddens, and, at the top of West Nile Street, opposite Buchanan Street Railway Station, my 107 would stop for the clippie to change the overhead wire points. These were known to trolleybus professionals as 'the frogs', because the section of the overhead switch where the wires went in different directions looked like a splayed frog's legs, and the term is still used in relation to tramway and railway points.

To frog change, platform staff used a three-foot-long wooden pole, topped with a brass hook, which inserted into a large, metal ring at the bottom of a wire running up a traction pole, to connect with the frog pull mechanism. A good chug changed the frogs, and once the driver saw the lights in a box on a pole ahead change from left to right, he went ahead.

That was done carefully, as per the rule book, for woe betide the driver who notched up too fast below the frogs and dewired. He would have to report the mishap on a form specially printed for the purpose, be interviewed by an inspector, and, if found to be at fault, could face a couple of days of suspension without pay.

On the morning in question, sitting on my usual seat upstairs, the bus empty after dropping all its office-bound passengers, and with the smoke clearing, I suddenly noticed one of the tie bars hanging down from the frogs, while the clippie was already making her way to give them a hearty chug with her pole.

What was I to do as a schoolboy in a world in which clippies were respected if not feared? If I let the trolley go ahead, there would be a spectacular dewirement, but, if I committed the cardinal sin of pressing the bell to alert the driver as a mere passenger, and a 15 year-old one at that, I would probably be skinned alive. But, I did press it, three times, the emergency stop signal, just as I could hear the thump of the clippie jumping back on board, the clatter of the frog pole being stowed below the stairs, and the hollow thud from the cab as the driver dropped the handbrake, holding the bus on the hill on one notch of power.

Suddenly, he slammed on the brakes with a great hiss of air, and the words' "What the f---?" could be heard from the cab, followed by footsteps coming up the stairs, where I was now standing.

"Whit are ye up tae, son?" he bellowed. "Interfering wi' ma trolley's a serious offence." I pointed to the frogs ahead of the bus and said: "There's part of the frogs hanging down I wanted to stop you dewiring."

Driver and clippie made their way to the front window and marvelled at the sight before them. "Son," said the driver, "ye've saved me a lot of trouble, so ye hiv. Well done. Now gie me yer name, address and school fur ma report."

After I did, I baled out as I was going to be late for Mass, which we had every day before lessons started, prayer before torture, as some said, as the trolley had another few minutes to run to reach Maitland Street terminus. I lingered just long enough to see the driver waving down a 105 behind, pull out the long, bamboo pole from under the rear platform, fish about aloft to bring the trolley booms down, and stow them under the hooks on the rear deck dome.

Until the overhead line department arrived in their tower wagon to repair the frogs, all the trolleys passing the spot would have to lower their booms, and move slowly past the spot on the traction batteries fitted to every trolleybus in Glasgow to let them run slowly for a limited distance independently of the wires. After that, it was stop again, to fish out the bamboo pole and place the trolleys back on the wires, an art which called for considerable skill, and kept the trolleybus crews quite fit, too.

In those days there was no cab radio and there were no mobile phones, but Glasgow Corporation Transport had a network of what were called traction phones, situated in green-painted locked boxes on pedestals, and with the letters 'GCT' on the doors. Drivers were issued with a key, also reputed to fit the locks on GCT staff cludgies, (Glaswegian slang for toilets) which opened the door to the phone, and were able to contact their home garage or head office for help. Our driver would have accessed the nearest traction phone in Cowcaddens, and a tower wagon crew would have been despatched from the overhead line department, housed in the old horse tram stables at Coplawhill, with repairs done as quickly as possible.

From my trolley home, that day, I could see that the frogs were repaired, and settled down in my front seat on the upper deck, to

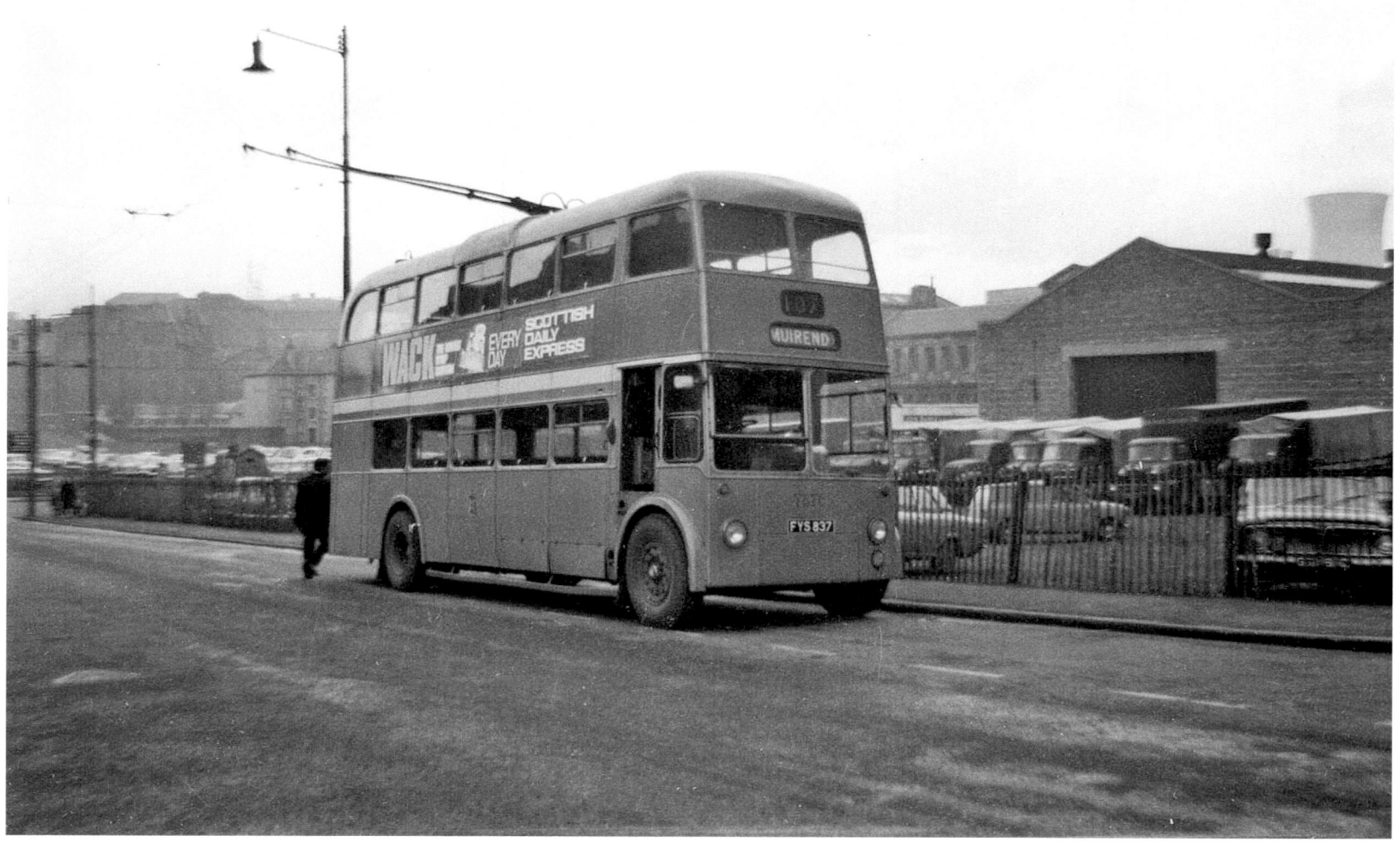

Journey's end on the way to school. TB76 waits its time at Maitland Street terminus on Saturday 4th February 1967. When Hugh started using the terminus, there were tenements all the way down the street, but these had been demolished by 1967, revealing the cooling tower of the Corporation's Pinkston Power Station, which generated electricity for the trolleybuses.

Hugh Dougherty

enjoy the journey. I was the only passenger until we filled up as we went down the town, picking up early office finishers, who settled down to read their *Evening Citizen* or *Evening Times*, and ladies completing a day of shopping, who boarded at the end of Sauchiehall Street on West Nile Street, or Glassford Street's Argyle Street stop, handy for Marks & Spencer's. Leaving Maitland Street at 4.11pm, I would be home in Battlefield, just after 4.30 pm, and, as often as not, TB121, would be on the shift, this bus having a traction motor which sounded uncannily like a tram, so that it became a favourite of mine.

It was on that run home, too, that I got to know Joe Doherty- no relation (!)- a Hampden Garage conductor, who struck up a conversation, as he lifted my fare at Maitland Street. He'd spotted my green school uniform and spoke in a soft Donegal accent, which I recognised, and we quickly established mutual links and connections. Joe was from Rathmullan, and had come over to Glasgow to work on the trolleys several years previously. He wore his green uniform as per the rule book and his hat like a guardsman, took enormous pride in the job and was delighted to find out that I was interested in the trolleys.

A friendship resulted and, over the years, Joe was able to answer the many questions that I had about the trolleys, firing up my quest for more in an age when there was no internet and information came from books or talking to people who knew! He was a gentleman and a credit to himself, Donegal and Glasgow Corporation Transport, and one of many Donegal men and women working out of Hampden Garage. It was handy for Govanhill where many lived as the community became established, and moved into better housing out of the Gorbals. Years later, after Joe died, I discovered that he also owned what he called 'a wee farm' in Donegal, and used to attend the Royal Highland Show every year. Joe was more than a trolleybus conductor!

Now, trolleybuses are controlled by two pedals, in the shape of an accelerator and a brake, but, on a trolley, the power pedal was worked by the left foot and the brake by the right. That was because early trolleybuses evolved from trams, and trams always had, and, generally still do, their power controller worked by the left hand, and the brake by the right, dating from

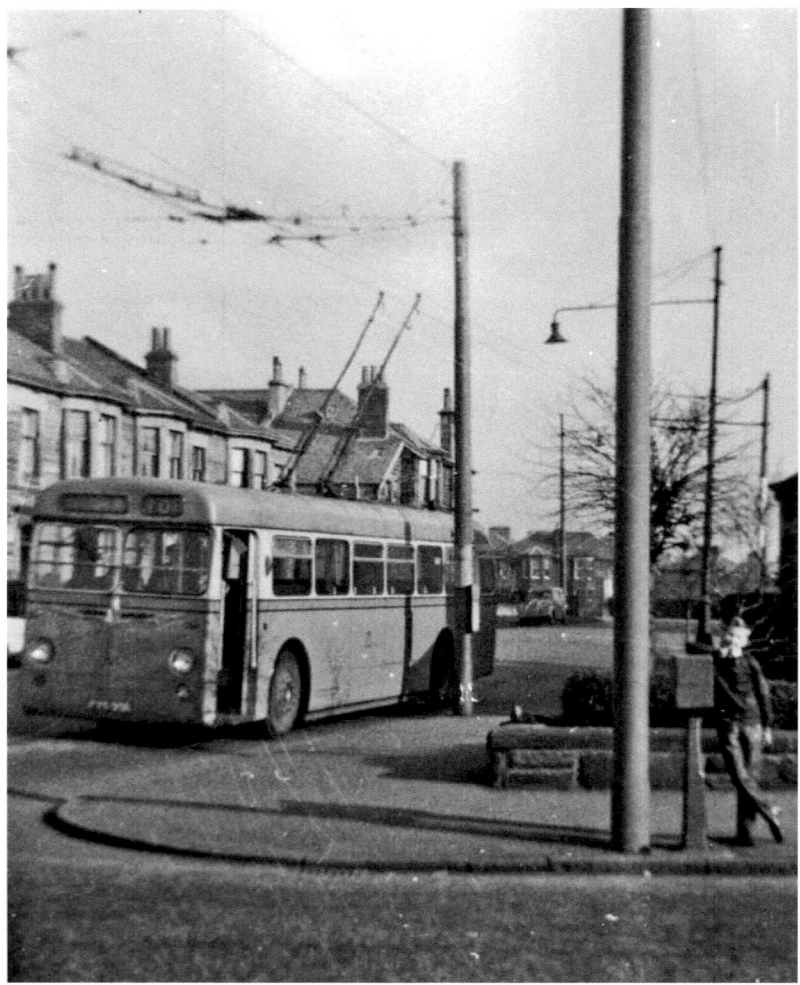

One of the BUT single deckers of 1958 sits at Mount Florida Terminus, before setting off for Paisley Road Toll in March 1965, while a school pal leans on the traction phone provided for trolleybus emergencies.

Hugh Dougherty

the days before air and rheostatic brakes. Drivers had to use the brute force of their right arm to wind on their mechanical brake handle to stop the tram.

The left foot power pedals of the trolleys gave rise to a nickname for Hampden as the 'left footer garage', a reference not just to the fact that trolleybus drivers use their left foot to go, but that there were many 'left footers', Glasgow slang for Catholics, at Hampden, because of the Donegal connection. One former trolleybus clippie whom I know, arrived from Donegal in the early 1960s, went to the transport department's head office in Bath Street for her interview, passed with flying colours, and was told by the inspector that she was being sent to 'the left footer garage'.

She duly reported to Hampden, and she married her regular driver, who also hailed from across the Irish Sea. Hampden had the reputation of being a happy garage, and when the next wave of immigrants, recruited by GCT from the Pakistani community, arrived in the early 1960s, integration was good, Joe's best line being that at Hampden, most crews came from Donegal or Bengal!

A few days after the frogs incident, I was summoned to the heidie's office. What had I done? I didn't own a shortie, white raincoat, my hair wasn't cut square at the back, and my trousers weren't less than 16 inches wide at the turn-ups, the holy trinity of Father Tracey's crusade against what he described as the excesses of teenage fashion of the 60s. Nor had I been near the convent school across the road….

But, despite my fears, he told me that he'd had a call from the director of education, who'd had a call from the director of transport, local government was joined up in the 1960s, saying that I'd saved a trolleybus from serious damage thanks to my smart thinking. Father Tracey praised a very relieved me for once! As a Jesuit, he worked out that I was a trolleybus enthusiast, but he assured me he'd come across worse during his teaching career and encouraged me to learn more.

Meanwhile, sweeping to and from school on the 107, daily, I determined to see the rest of the system, and, by judicious pocket money saving, I made it up the Garngad on the 101 all the way to Riddrie and out to Rutherglen, through the heart of a then still-intact Gorbals, all soot-blackened tenements, gas-lit side streets, and scary, spit-and-sawdust pubs. I felt a wee bit insecure as my six-wheeler hummed up the High Street, through a now long-obliterated Townhead, complete with a cinema, library, shops and tenements, to Royston Road and up the Garngad, where local folk just seemed a bit tougher than the douce ladies who frequented our 107!

I got to know the 106 between Millerston and Paisley Road Toll, as every Wednesday we went to the school's Millerston playing fields and, after suffering on the cold and muddy pitches, I would board a very foreign-feeling 106 which lived at, to me, slightly-mysterious Govan Garage. Off we would speed along Cumbernauld Road, past picturesque Hogganfield Loch, by forbidding-looking HM Prison Barlinnie, down into then-ungentrified Dennistoun, home to pop star Lulu, (did she ever travel on a 106?) with truly local shops, long before planners came up with 20-minute neighbourhoods, and through the Orange heartlands of Bridgeton Cross. I never did get off there!

The 106 was a very busy route with lots of short-trip passengers, and we crossed the 101/102 wires at Ballater Street, before inching along under the railway bridge leading to St Enoch Station, with the trolleys making a peculiar scratching noise as they ran under the metalwork of the bridges, for the wires were carried in insulated, wooden troughs. We would stop at busy Gorbals Cross, where there was a complex overhead wire layout to savour, with square crossings of the 107 and 105 routes and a set of frogs to allow rush hour specials from Hampden to take up journeys on the 106.

From there, it was down through a very intact Tradeston, to Paisley Road Toll, where I baled out to catch a 108, quite exotically, a single decker, for Mount Florida. These trolleybuses were fast and lively riding, their main drawback seeming to be that their hopper vent windows had a nasty habit of falling open as the bus sped along, with the clippie cursing as she slammed them shut for the umpteenth time on her shift!

The 108 took you up though the wealthy, Victorian suburb of Pollokshields, and the long, single deckers, looked quite regal under the wires on Shields Road, before gaining the tenements of Govanhill and negotiating the square crossing with the 107s at

Victoria Road, joining the 105 wires at Cathcart Road, and running smartly to Mount Florida. They emitted a characteristic 'hollow' sound from the traction motor as the driver pressed his left foot down to feel the top notches on the power pedal.

When I was about 15, I resolved to take Father Tracey's advice and learn more about the trolleybuses. A visit after school, to Stirling's Library engineering section, yielded an electric traction handbook, which taught me everything there was to know about trolleybuses. I learned why the traction poles which held up the overhead wires, weren't planted straight, but were 'raked' backwards, so that, when the span wires, which held up the trolley wires and their insulators, were attached, the poles were pulled true.

No decent overhead line man would have wanted that, and certainly not in Glasgow, which prided itself in its knowledge of traction engineering, with experience built up from the earliest electric trams of 1898 onwards. I also learned how to site frogs and to calculate the number of span wires needed for curves of different radii. This was practical and solid geometry which they never told you about at school!

The white painted bands on poles that you saw from your trolleybus every half mile or so along the route, were also explained, as section gaps, to insulate one section of wires from the others, and also to feed power into the overhead. The white bands reminded drivers to shut off power when passing under them, and then to notch up again after. This all gave me a whole new level of trolleybus appreciation, and I kept that book out for months.

I kept travelling to and from school by the 107 until the route was axed on 4th February 1967, being replaced by a dreaded diesel, the 67 bus. Of course, I had to stay loyal to the trolley, so I caught the 105 from round the corner from us on Holmlea Road and baled out in Cowcaddens, sad in the knowledge that the 105 itself was due to be withdrawn on 27th May 1967. Glasgow had decided to scrap the trolleys, despite the buses I used dally being built in 1957-58, with years of life in them.

The city fathers were imbued with a passion for the motor car, despite the fact that just 20 percent of Glaswegians owned one, and electric street traction with its poles and wires, which spoke reassuringly of permanency to passengers, and a hindrance to planners, was to be swept away in the orgy of destruction which saw whole swathes of the city flattened to make way for a brave new world of motorways, which had no place for the trolleybus.

As far as Glasgow Corporation was concerned, the replacement diesel buses would just have to fight for road space with cars, and, of course, their routes could be chopped and changed as demolition of areas such as the Garscube Road, Townhead and Gorbals, all traditional haunts of trolleybuses, went on apace.

As Councillor Willie Lee transport committee chairman put it in January 1967: "The trolleybuses will be withdrawn as soon as possible. The redevelopment of the city will affect a number of trolleybus routes." Redevelopment, of course, was the primary reason, and here was no mention of increased pollution in those days by substituting diesel buses for the trolleys. The expected £975,000 raised from selling off the trolleys and their fittings for scrap represented a massive waste of hardly life-expired public assets, just as with the earlier orgy of tram scrapping which had taken place five years previously.

It was all so short-sighted and the results can be seen today, 60 years later, as public transport continues to take second place in Glasgow, while there are vague mutterings about what is loosely described as the "Glasgow Metro". But, if one thing is clear, it is that the trolleybus, in its modern guise, as found in cities across the globe won't be included, even though its silence, the vary aspects that earned it the name of Silent Death in Glasgow, is much prized in many cities today.

Glasgow, I'm afraid to say, was permanently dewired on 27th May 1967 when the last 105 left Queen's Cross terminus. If the system had lasted a decade or so more, someone might have recognised the environmental benefits of the trolleys, and they would be playing a key role in keeping Glasgow moving today.

If I learned one lesson from travelling to and from school under the wires daily, it's this: trolleybuses are reliable fast, efficient, non-polluting and silent. What wouldn't we give for a 107 making its silent way up the town today?

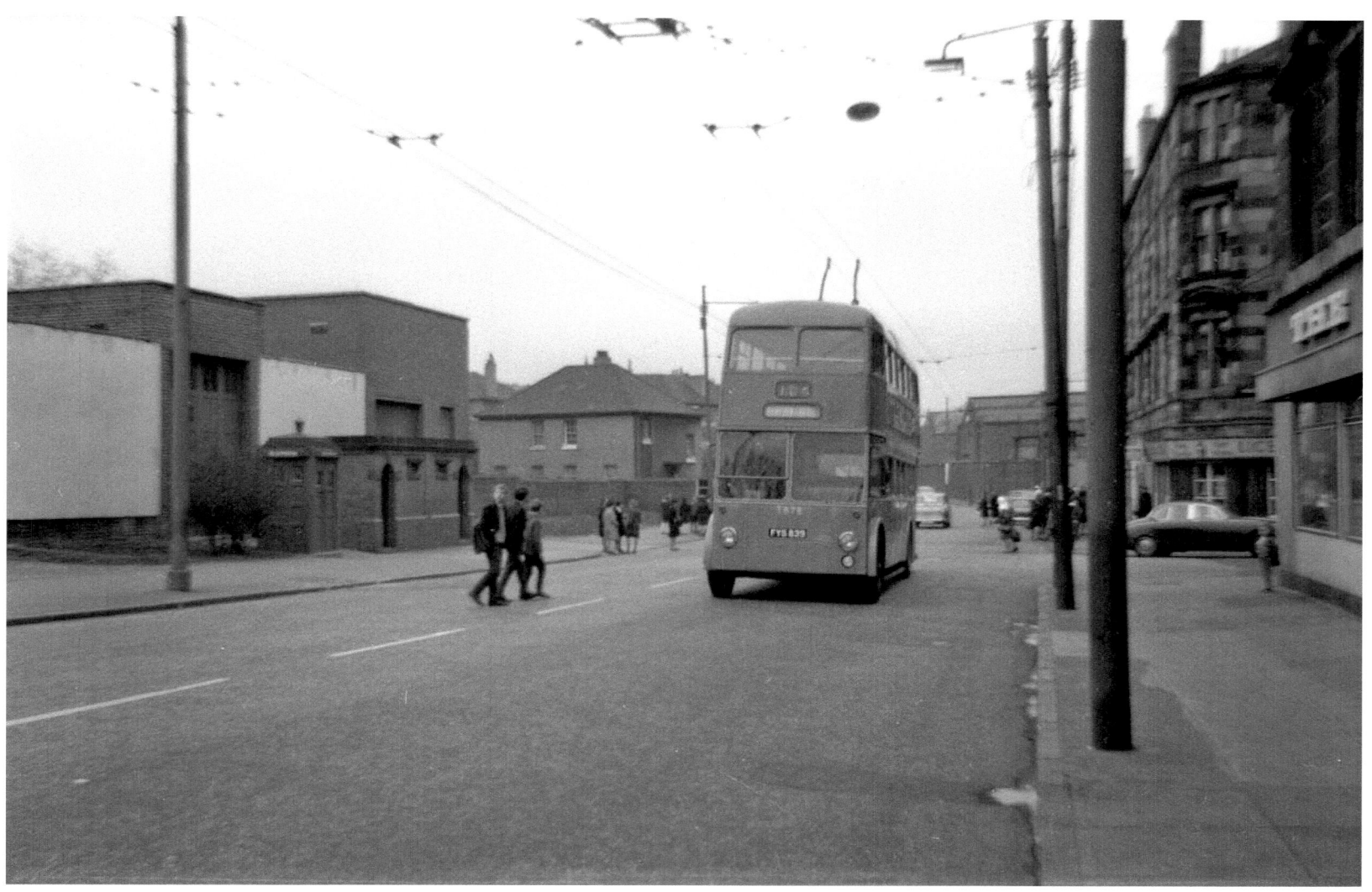

Holyrood Secondary School pupils dice with silent death on Aikenhead Road, in the best traditions of Glaswegian pedestrians, in March 1967, while TB78 makes for Hampden Garage. The trolley is about to negotiate the frogs for Polmadie turning circle. *Hugh Dougherty*

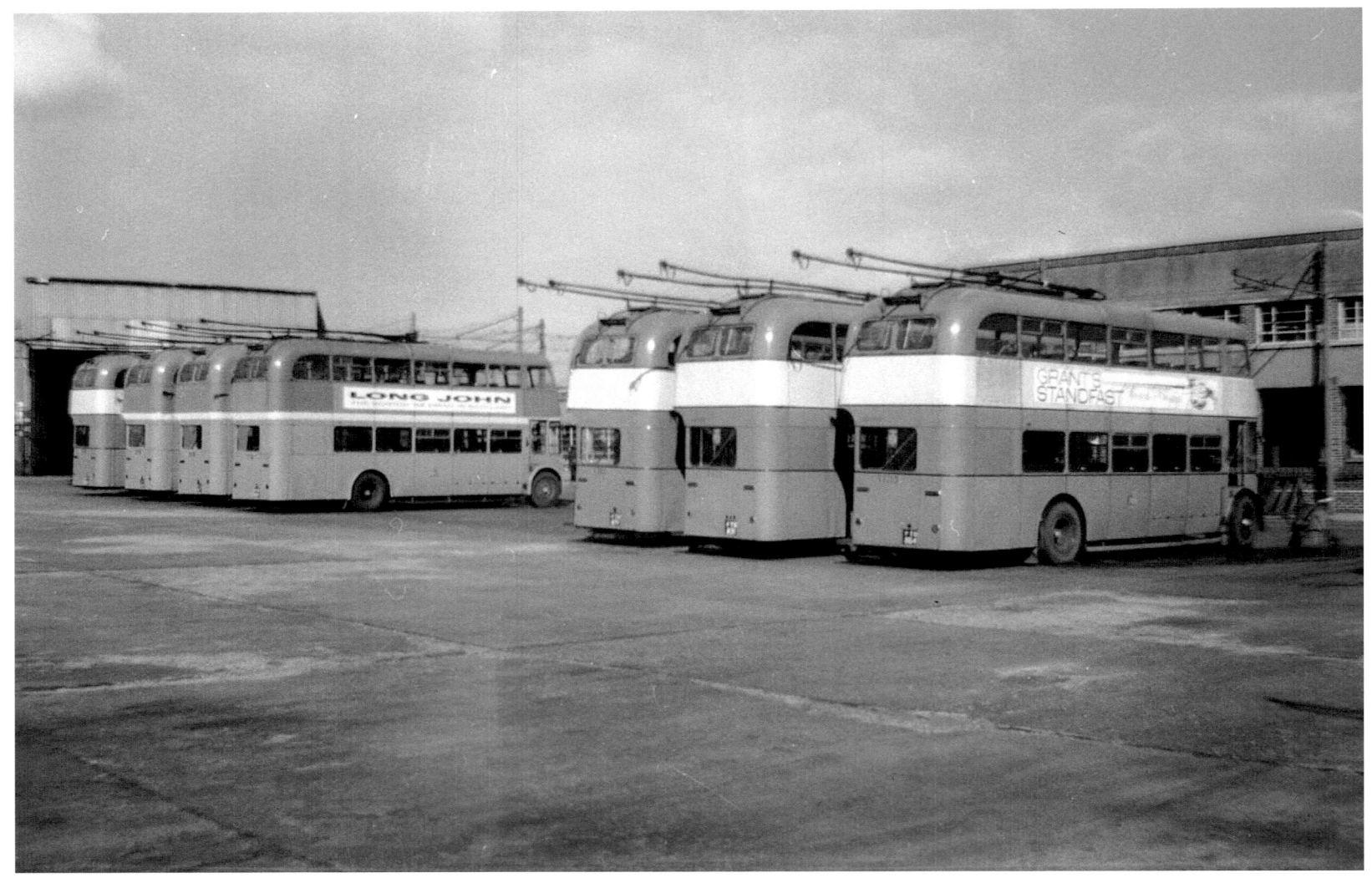

The ramped, open air floor at Hampden, with trolleys awaiting their next turn of duty in March 1967. The garage always turned its trolleys out well, right up to the closure. *Hugh Dougherty*

Hampden Garage – The Holy of Holies

Standing at the doors of Langside Tram Depot with my mother, and staring in wonder at the lines of trams, as only a five year-old can, the gateman told us that the depot was going to be converted for trolleybuses. The Langside trolleys would whizz up the hills to serve the rapidly-expanding, Castlemilk housing scheme which was eating up most of the countryside beyond Croftfoot.

That rumour persisted locally, but, when the trams were ousted, the brick-built depot was converted to a diesel bus garage. Its buses spent their lives struggling noisily, blasting out diesel exhaust fumes, up the hills to the isolated, new housing. Castlemilk never enjoyed the benefits of swift and silent electric traction, even though a further rumour held that trolleybus cable ducts had been laid.

Trolleybuses in Glasgow first ran out of Larkfield Bus Garage, when introduced in 1949, while they also operated out of Dennistoun Tram Depot for a time, and, when the 106 route replaced the number 7 trams in 1958, they dug in at Govan Depot, where they ran alongside both trams and buses for some years.

However, the real holy of holies for me, was Hampden Garage. Opened in 1950, and extended in 1957, Hampden, housed 147 trolleybuses at the height of its powers in 1960, the epicentre of trolleybus operations, for me. Sitting in the shadow of Hampden Park itself, this was a place I just had to visit to find out more about the trolleys, especially when not on the streets.

One Saturday in 1964, I plucked up the courage, when, with two school pals, I asked the gateman if we could have a look round. He said we could, and, parked up the back were some of the original single deckers, while most of the six-wheeler Daimlers, the TDS, as they were known to crews, had been withdrawn, and were parked, awaiting their fate. It was fascinating to see the trolleys close up, and, after an hour or so, when we had been on every bus in the place, we left. I vowed to return to find out even more.

Hampden was flanked on one side by post-war prefabs and 1920s-built cottage flats on the other, and the garage was something of an adventure, open-air playground for the local weans when no one was looking. A family friend, now a respected retired head teacher, revealed that when she was growing up in Curling Crescent in the 1950s, she and her pals would swarm over their back garden wall and invade the garage, and the kids from the prefabs would do the same.

"We would play at trolleybuses on the trolleybuses," she recalled. "It was easy not to be seen as the out-of-service trolleys were parked up at the back, far from the garage offices, so we could do what we liked until, that is, we were eventually chucked out by staff. We came back, of course, and kids playing on the trolleys became part of local life and folklore. When I went on to secondary school at Our Lady & St Francis in Charlotte Street, I travelled by trolleybus every day, and it was a great service."

The garage also played a key role on match days at Hampden, with every bus that could move out on service to carry the massive

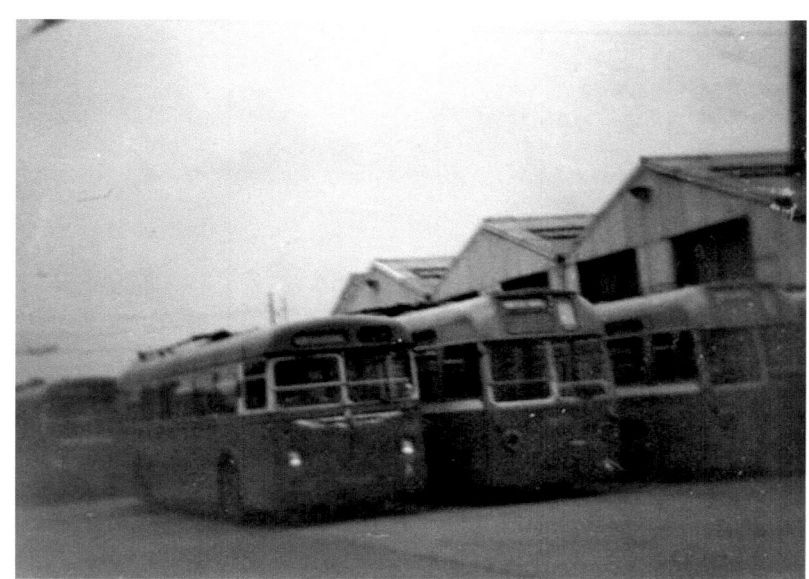

My first Glasgow trolleybus picture taken with a very cheap camera in January 1964, shows single deckers of 1958 and 1953 parked at the back of Hampden Garage's workshops, where they were ideal for the local kids to play on out of sight of the staff!

Hugh Dougherty

crowds of fans of those days to and from the stadium. Once emptied of trolleys, the garage apron was used as a car park, although car drivers had to be reminded to set their handbrakes firmly, as the whole garage area was ramped downwards towards Aikenhead Road to aid trolleybus shunting when off the wires.

And the trolleys brought fans from the centre of the city for cup finals and internationals. I can remember watching some Rangers fans from Belfast where trolleybuses were painted red-and-white, swearing eloquently and giving the passing Glasgow buses the Vicky, because they equated their green, cream and orange livery with the Irish tricolour. Home-grown Rangers fans, some of whom used the 106 to get close to Ibrox Park, didn't seem to notice!

On Wednesday 30th November 1966, my wee green book tells me, I presented myself at the garage gate, and asked the shunter, a kindly and elderly man dressed in overalls, topped by a brass-buttoned GCT driver's tunic and a non-uniform bunnet, if I could have a look round. As it was St Andrew's Day, we got a half-day off school, so what better than to do a little trolleybus exploration...

He duly admitted me, we had a chat and then he said, to my astonishment: "How would you like to drive a trolleybus, son?" pointing to TB46, which was sitting in the wash bay. I couldn't believe my luck, and so it was into the cab, with himself sitting on the contactor box and me in the driving seat, as he took me through the starting drill.

It was a case of main switch on, select the forward position on the control box, switch, put on the compressor and motor generator switches, and wait for the brake pressure to come up. Before it did, a metal flag, with the letters STOP perforated on it, stood firm in front of the windscreen, and you couldn't move until it had dropped into its slot.

"Now," said the shunter: "Left foot on the left pedal and press it down to strike the first power notch. You'll feel the bus wanting to move forward, and, when you do, ease off the hand brake, and she won't roll back."

I was amazed to feel the trolley, silently and seemingly effortlessly, move forward, and, as I struck the second power notch, which you could feel through the pedal, our speed went up, just as I realised that I had to steer what seemed an enormously-wide bus, too. Then there were the wires to contend with, and I was told to keep my left shoulder under the outer wire to avoid dewiring as we made our way round the garage overhead circuit.

The trolleybus was wonderfully free-running, and the steering, despite being in the days long before power steering, was responsive, even though it needed several turns of the large steering wheel to change direction. No wonder a trolleybus driver was tired at the end of his shift. This was a very physical job, and I wasn't even having to look in the mirrors or deal with other traffic. But what an experience for a 16 year old!

Beside myself with excitement, I suddenly realised that I was being watched from the garage apron by the superintendent, who was assessing my driving skills, and, when he stopped, he insisted that I take the trolleys down, "to see if you're a real driver and if you've had your porridge this morning!"

This was a real test of skill and stamina, for, besides having to pull the long, bamboo pole, from under the bus, I had to hold this aloft as it wobbled precariously above me, insert its hook into the ring at the end of the trolley, and haul it down from the wire against the strong, upward pull of its spring, before fastening it under the storage hook at the end of the upper deck.

I'd seen crews do this with ease, but it was far harder than it looked, and, as a crowd of off-duty and spare drivers and conductors had gathered by this time to watch my attempt, there were shouts of "eat some more porridge, son!" and "Ye'll never make a trolley driver!", as I was nearly pulled off my feet, before I took the strain. Let's just say, that some 15 minutes after, to ironic applause from the small crowd of green-uniformed figures, I had finally both trolleys off the wires and stowed. It was quite a lesson in real life.

The superintendent, a Mr Connelly, and remember that adults didn't have first names in those days, kind man that he was, showed me round the workshops, where, TB109 was being repainted by hand, as Hampden always took a pride in turning out its trolleybuses, while in the stores there was a mercury arc rectifier, looking like a giant light bulb, as used in the sub stations that fed power into the trolleybus wires, to convert AC to DC traction current. It has been bought from London Transport when it scrapped its trolleys in 1962, and held as a spare.

Mr Connelly shared my sorrow that the trolleybuses were to be scrapped in six months' time, and felt that a very poor decision had

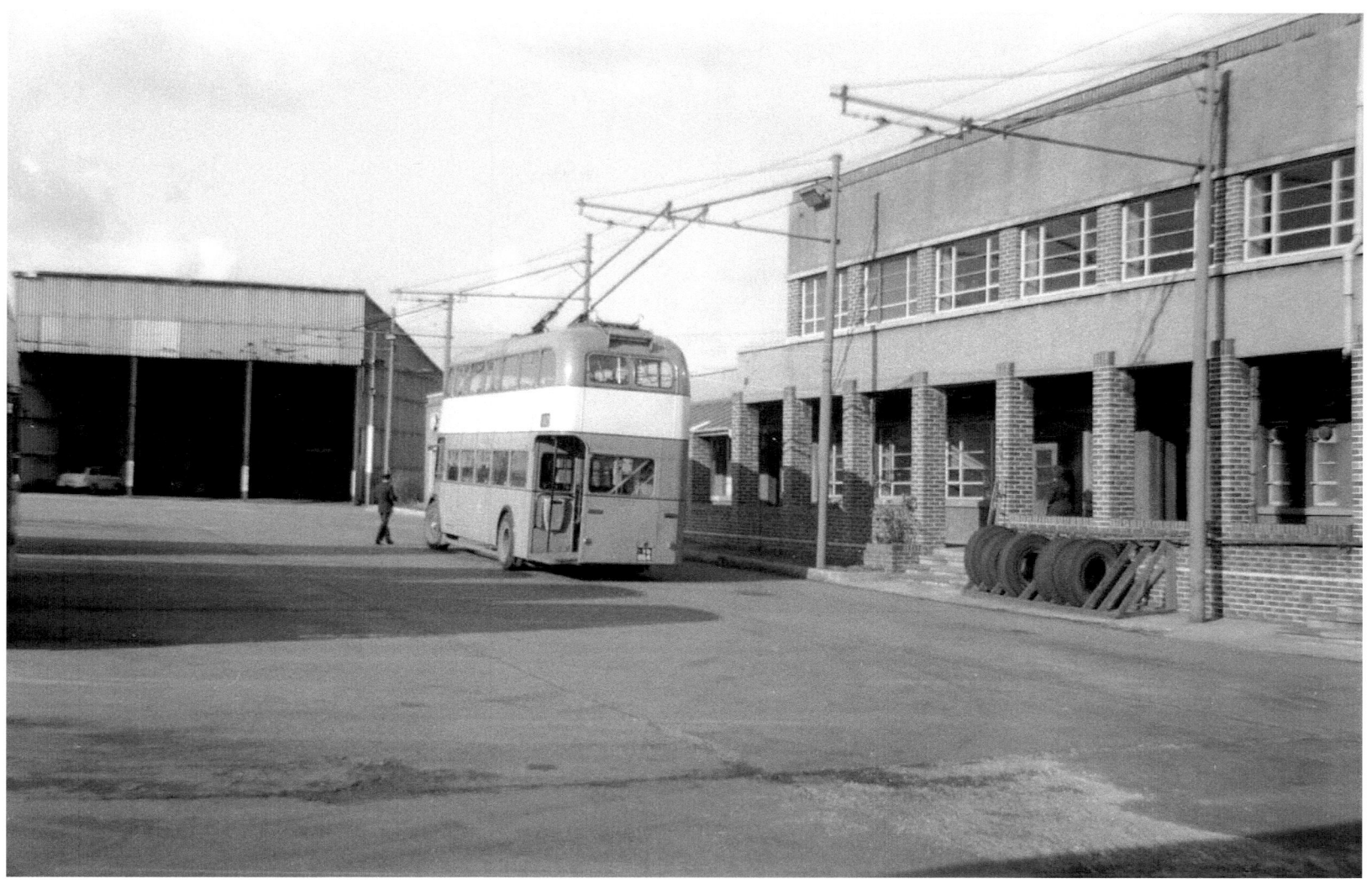

It was fascinating to get behind the scenes at Hampden and the overhead wires, supported on what were known as bracket arms outside the depot offices, were the ones I drove trolleys round under the shunter's eagle eye.

Hugh Dougherty

been made. Recognising my genuine interest in them, he sent me home with some souvenirs in the shape of a destination blind, BUT plate off a wheel hub and a frog pole. I can't repeat what my parents said as I came in the front door with them, but the blind, with white letters on a green background, as were all the first Glasgow trolleybus screens, was later donated to Sandtoft Trolleybus Museum near Doncaster. After being used by my late parents as a window pole, the frog changer lives in our loft today, proof positive that I a 16 year-old me really did drive TB46 that day so long ago and that Glasgow did once have trolleybuses.

I was back at Hampden a couple of time more before the end, with my school pal, Paul Adams, whom I realised was of a similar persuasion to myself, when I noticed that he was reading an Ian Allan booklet, *British Bus Fleets*, Glasgow, under the desk, during a science class, and, despite him being a diesel, Albion man at heart, he was game for a close look at the trolleys.

Paul, who went on to become my brother-in- law, a founder member of the Albion Preservation Trust, and a stalwart of the Glasgow Vintage Vehicle Trust, was with me on 25th May 1967, when, two days, before the last trolleybus ran, we rode up to Hampden behind the garage tow wagon from Larkfield Bus Works on newly-overhauled TBS21.

It had been bought by the National Trolleybus Association for preservation in England, incredibly, using S&H Pink Stamps, a trading, promotional scheme of the sixties. TBS21 was to run a special tour for NTA members on the last day of the system, but, after some to-and-froing down south the bus returned to Glasgow, including storage at Bridgeton Garage, but the trolley was finally scrapped as no one really wanted it by then, because of its neglected condition.

My wee green book also tells me that I last drove at Hampden on Monday 8th May 1967, when I did a couple of circuits with TB69 and parked her, quite expertly, my shunter friend told me, and I was chuffed. My parents thought that this wasn't the best use of my afternoon off school to study for my impending Highers, but it was interesting, when, five years later, in 1972, I passed my PSV test to drive with Western SMT as a student bus driver, and I have to say that none of the Leyland and Daimler diesels I drove that summer came anywhere near a trolleybus in terms of sophistication or smoothness.

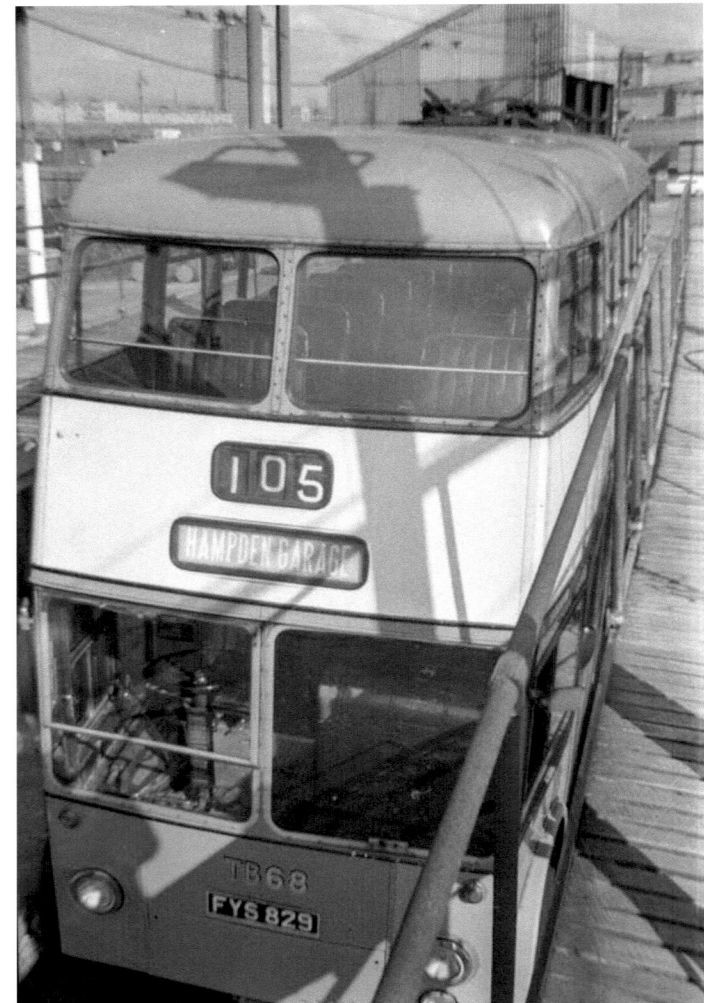

Sitting in the wash at Hampden is TB68, driven out under the shunter's supervision (!) later that afternoon, by Hugh on 30th March 1967.

Hugh Dougherty

Just for the record, I did pass my Highers, and, each day that I sat them, I was confident that my trusty 105 would get me to the school on time, even though I preferred watching the passing trolleybuses rather than having a last swot as we whined up steep West Nile Street, which, as late as 1964, was still home to horses and carts making their way to and from Buchannan Street (railway) Goods Station.

My last visit to Hampden was on 27th May 1967, when I joined the Scottish Tramway Museum Society's Last Trolleybus tour of the system, using TB78 and TB123. The once-bustling garage was a sad place that Saturday, with most crews signing off for the last time, the depot canteen already closed, and strong opinions being expressed by drivers, clippies and conductors that their transfer to diesels at Larkfield and Langside garages, was not something they were looking forward to.

Hampden Garage was a happy place, and it was sad to see it go. The trolleys were removed with unseemly haste the day after the last run, for temporary storage at Ibrox Bus Garage, before they were carted off for scrapping, and the site was used by the Corporation lighting department for a few years.

I did, once, attempt a visit to Govan Garage, home of the trolleys on the 106, where they shared space, initially with trams, and, later with diesels, but never made it inside. Govan trolleys were never kept as well as Hampden buses, although today the garage offices have survived as flats and you can still make out the carved letters "GCT" on the gatepost.

Today, the Hampden site, my holy of holies, sits largely empty, apart from the area beside Aikenhead Road, which acts, in the mind of transport planners, at least, as a park-and-ride facility, which few car drivers seem inclined to use. With its ramped floor still there with memories of what might have been, had the wires been extended to Castlemilk at one extremity, and to Milngavie from Queen's Cross at the other, as originally mooted, and the trolleybus system developed, rather than sacrificed, in homage to the private car, Hampden would still be paying a vital role in public transport provision today.

What a pity it is that the silent service itself was silenced at Hampden on 27th May 1967. If only the bare, concrete expanse of Hampden could talk, what stories of trolley days in Glasgow it might be able to tell.

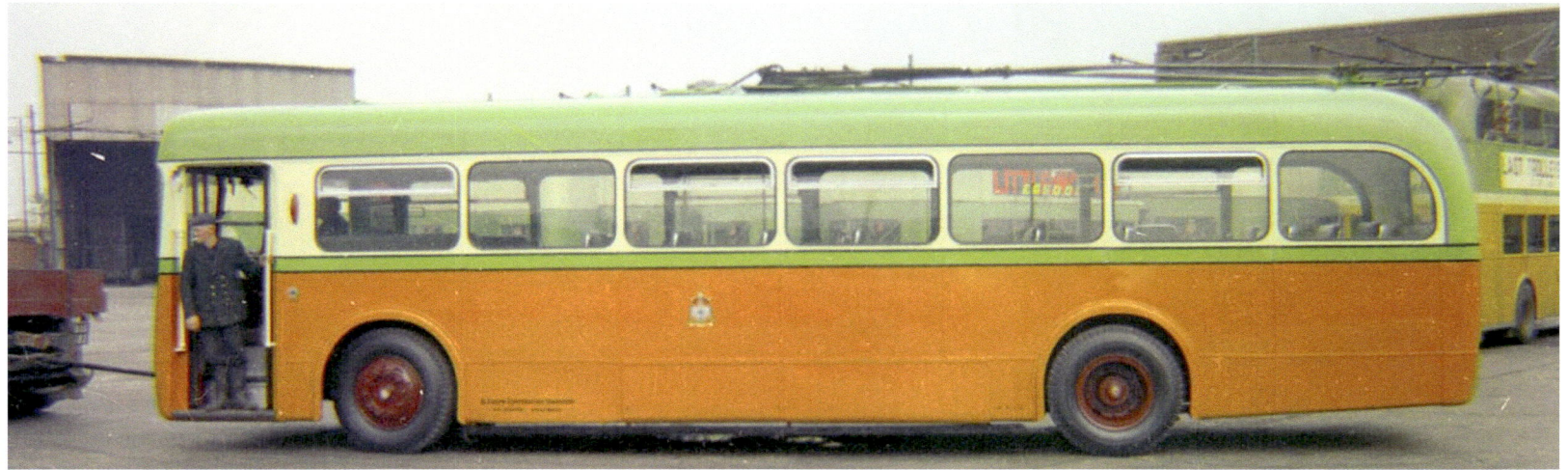

TBS 21, which was intended for preservation, was towed up to Hampden from Larkfield Bus Works on 25th May 1967, after a repaint. In the doorway is the shunter who let me drive trolleys. Note his old driver's tunic, cloth bunnet, wellies, and fag! *Hugh Dougherty.*

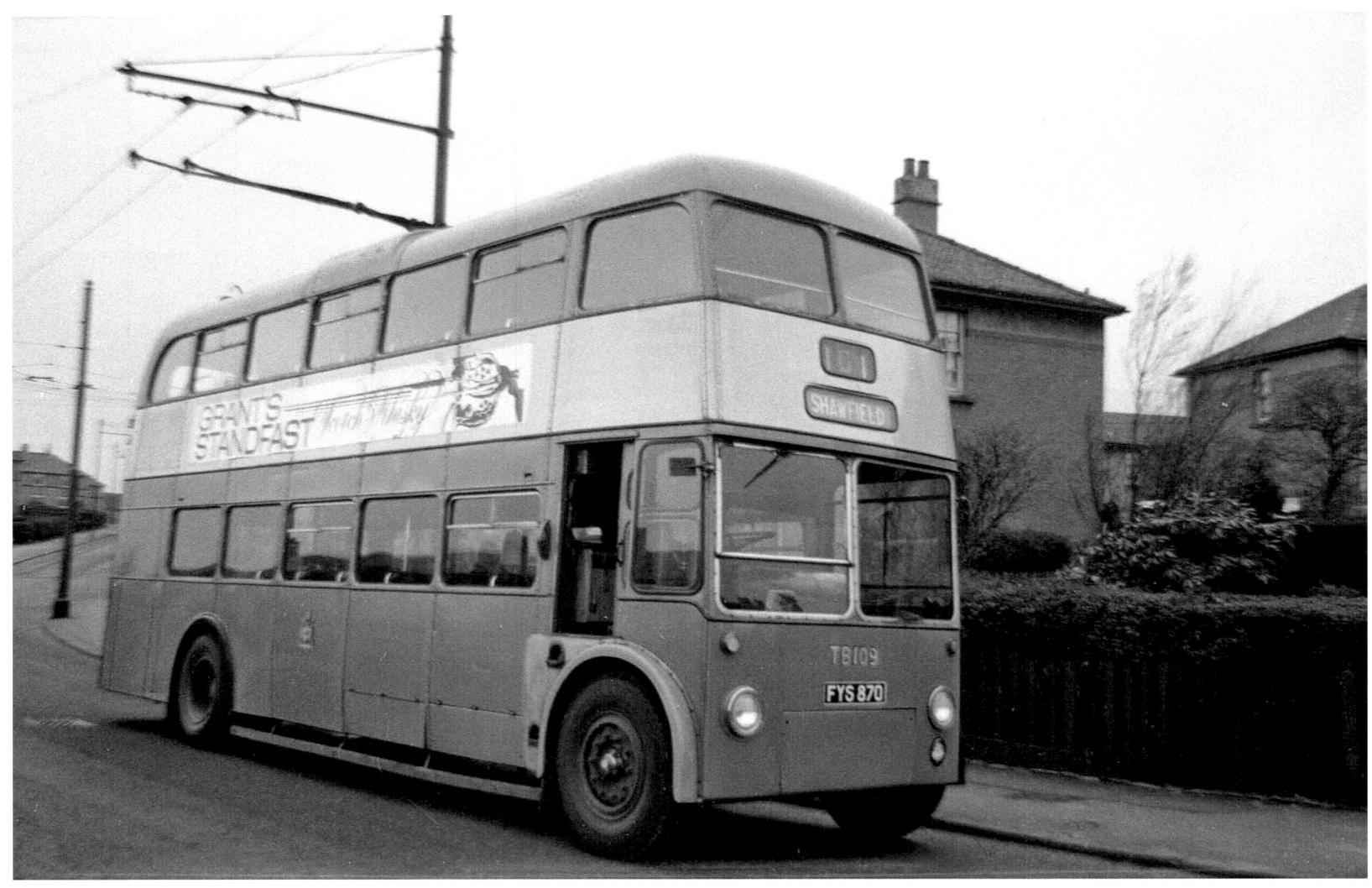

Out on the road, Hampden's trolleys always looked immaculate. On 29th April 1966, TB109, stands fast at Riddrie Terminus, ready to return to Shawfield destination for the 'dug specials'.

Hugh Dougherty

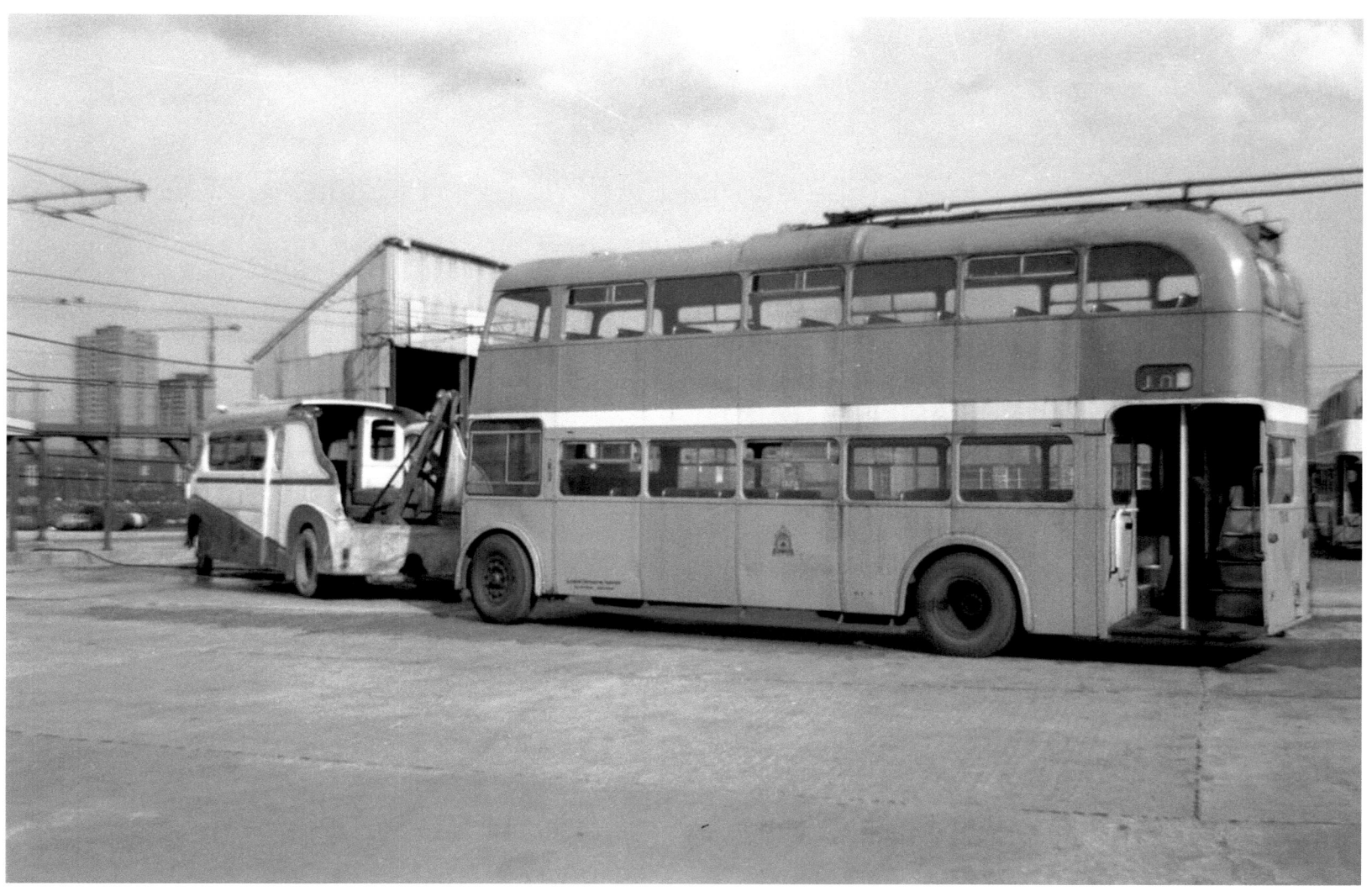

Just nine years-old, one of the BUT-built trolleys, is towed away from Hampden Garage to be scrapped by Dunsmore of Larkhall in April 1967. It was such a waste of money.

Hugh Dougherty

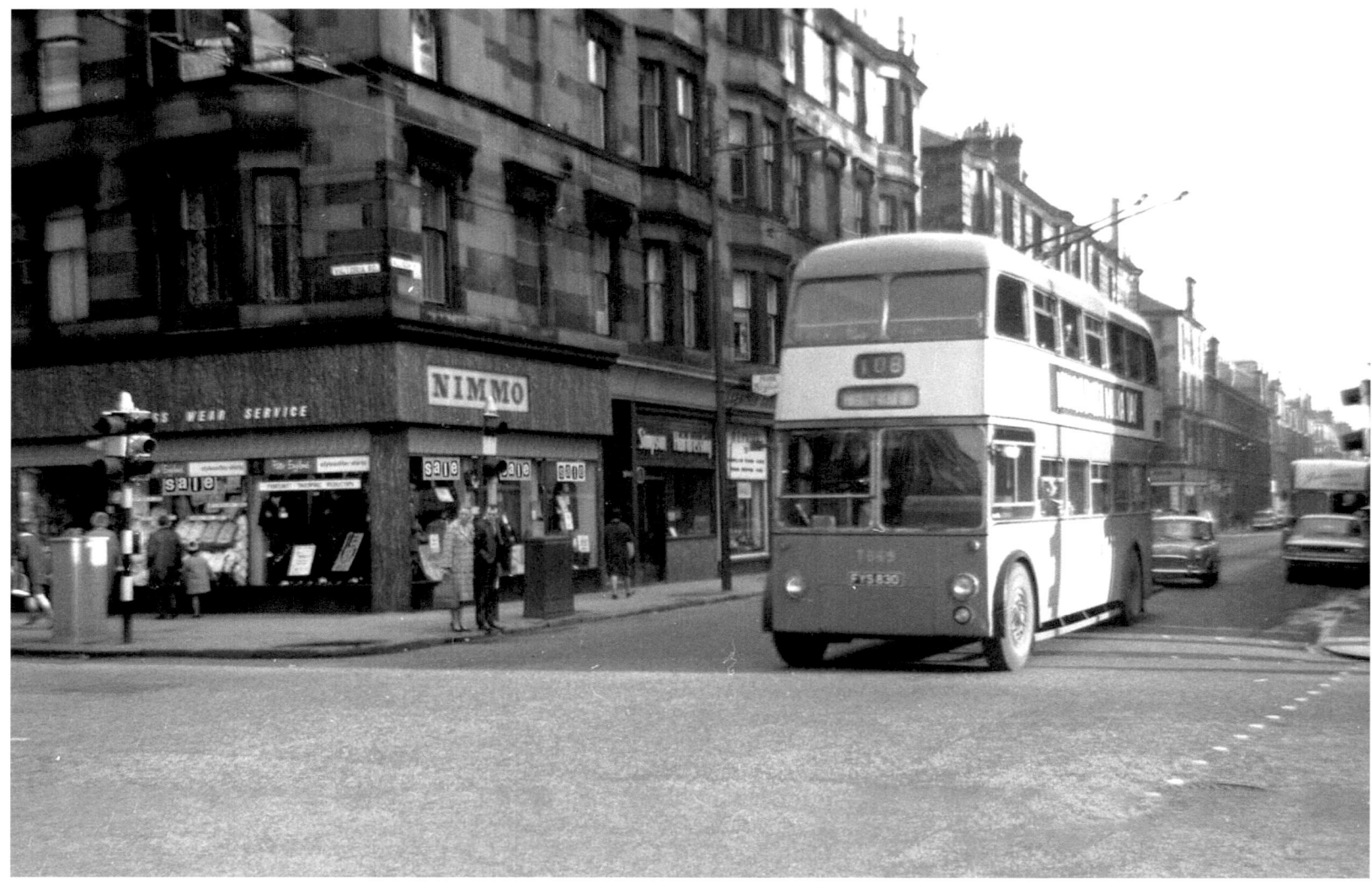

The junction of Victoria Road and Allison Street, where the Orange mace shorted out the trolley wires. TB69 crosses the 107 wires and Vicky Road, then a flourishing shopping avenue, in March 1966, for Paisley Road Toll. *Hugh Dougherty*

Star of Glasgow's Street Theatre

Glaswegians loved their theatres during trolleybus days and many would use the silent service in the evening to enjoy "The Five Past Eight Show", at the Alhambra, or to watch Francie and Josie's antics at the Pavilion. These two, loveable rogues would almost certainly have jumped on a 105 in their Cowcaddens, spiritual homeland!

Trolleybuses took passengers galore to Glasgow's many cinemas, to be found, then, in the city centre and suburbs, as TV hadn't yet killed them off, while Friday and Saturday night dancers, many looking for 'a lumber', Glaswegian for girl or boy friend, poured off the trolleys at Dennsitoun Palais or the Plaza at Eglinton Toll. The system also served Hampden Park, Cathkin Park, home of Third Lanark FC and Firhill, for Partick Thistle, where the 105 terminated just across the road. There was also Shawfield, where Clyde FC shared house room with a greyhound track. Race night punters came on what crews called 'the dug specials', on the 101, turning at Shawfield, so that trolleybuses played a key role in getting Glaswegians to leisure.

But it was on the routes themselves that the trolleybus starred in the street theatre so beloved of Glaswegians. High drama would be enacted in the evenings, and at weekends, at the end of Gorbals Main Street, home to the Citizens' Theatre, catering for the more erudite whose tastes were above variety shows and pantos, where the 105 and 107 wires split for Cathcart and Pollokshaws Roads. There, where the trolleybuses stopped for the clippie to change the frogs for 107s to branch off, followed by a careful, 5mph negotiation under a low railway bridge, the local weans, especially on light, summer evenings, and at weekends would pounce, desperate for a hudgie.

A hudgie is Glaswegian for a wean having a free 'hurl' or trip, on the back of a moving vehicle, and a trolley at Gorbals frogs was a gift that no self-respecting, wild, Gorbals wean could pass up. As the bus moved off, the urchins, all snottery noses, googly glasses, dirty faces, bravado and sheer cheek, would swarm onto the rear platform, swinging round the centre pole and handrails, while questioning the conductor's parentage.

Conductors and clippies dealt with this by using a range of non-rule book measures. Some yelled the clippie's cry of "C'moan, get aff! Others aimed a kick in the direction of the miscreants, and, in extreme circumstances, they would lay about the young offenders with the frog pole, allied with a string of curses. That usually did it – until the next trolley came along for boarding and the weans surged forward again.

From March onwards, when Glaswegians know winter's over, by spotting their first Orangeman of spring, Orange bands, in trolleybus days, as now, made their way onto the streets. I'll never forget being at the junction of Victoria Road and Allison Street, one Saturday morning in 1964, where the 107 crossed the 108, when an Orange walk came along, heading for Queen's Park. I'd been sent to pay our TV rental, as you did in those days, every week, and in cash, and stopped to watch the show.

The police, "Ra Polis", kept the traffic flowing around the banners, sashes, flutes, accordions and drums, while the loyal brethren marched along with their peculiar, short-stepped, swaggering gait. One band was halted on Victoria Road, to allow a 108 trolley, and a long tail of cars and lorries to cross, as they passed along Allison Street.

A real 'kick the Pope' outfit, the band, rather than march on the spot marking time, decided to give it laldy, swinging into "The Sash", with the big drummer dancing on the spot and hitting the picture of His Holiness on the drum skin with gusto. This inspired the mace bearer to treat the pavement audience to an expert display of mace throwing and twirling.

The red-white-and-blue mace went round his back, over his shoulders, and, then to the applause of the crowd accompanying the band along the pavement, up in the air, to be caught before it reached the ground. Up again it went, but this time, it managed to lodge itself, no pun intended, across the trolleybus wires, carrying 600 volts DC. The flute and drum music faded away as band members, marchers, Polis, crowd and mace thrower, alike, looked up in amazement as the mace emitted an impressive display of red, white and blue sparks, before partially melting and welding itself to the wires.

A woman, having a classic hing, that is, looking out of her first floor tenement window at street life below, leaning on a cushion, smoking a fag, with her hair in rollers under a headscarf, shouted down: "Serves youse right, ye Orange B------!" and immediately, two Polis disappeared up the close. She was yanked inside, and her window slammed shut. There was enough of an emergency to deal with.

The now maceless band, was signalled to march on, but a 107 trolleybus held in the traffic queue behind, wasn't so fortunate, as it now had no power. The melting mace, had shorted out the trolley wires, blowing the switches in a feeder box further up the road and cutting power to the section. A visit by an overhead line repair gang to remove the remains of the mace, replace a section of trolley wire and reset the feeder box switches was needed before route 107 returned to normal. That was such wonderful street theatre, especially as a green-white-and-orange trolleybus had to surrender its mobility to a red-white-and-blue mace!

'Huvin' a hing' was common in the less-well-off parts of the trolleybus routes, such as the Gorbals, or up the Garscube Road to Queen's Cross, or through Townhead, Govan and the Garngad, but, of course, no middle class matrons in Cathcart, Clarkston (Claerkston, as some pronounced it) or Muirend, would ever indulge in such an activity. But, it was the first floor window on a tenement on Cathcart Road, at the corner of Newlands Road, beside Cathcart Railway Bridge, on the 105, that was the epicentre of much street theatre one Saturday morning in early 1967.

I'd been to the Coupar Institute Library and was walking home, having just passed under the railway bridge, when I heard a mighty crack, and window glass showered down onto the pavement. A 105 rolled to a halt alongside me, its nearside trolley well off the wires and stuck through the now-glassless, first floor, flat window.

The driver had exceeded the speed restriction under the bridge, a notorious dewirement spot, where if the bus went too fast, a wave motion would be set up by the trolley booms, and one, or both would come off. This time, the offside one had stayed on, but the other had come off, and bounced off the underside of the bridge. As the bus came out from under the bridge, the trolley boom, swung towards the tenement, smashing the window, and, worse still, detached the heavy, metal trolleyhead, which flew across the kitchen in which the occupant, an elderly lady was sitting reading her paper.

The white-faced driver emerged from the cab and pulled out the bamboo pole from under the bus. He started trying to free the trolley boom which was enmeshed in lighting wires running between the street light poles, but stopped when someone came running down the close shouting: "There's a wee wummin in that hoose. Ye'll huv tae talk to her."

At this, the driver handed the bamboo pole, attached to the trolley boom, to his clippie, who had come off the platform for a look. "Haud this!", he told her, pressing the pole into her hands, but looked on in horror as the clippie, all five feet of her, and lightly built, was wheeched aloft by the upwards and powerful pull of the trolley which suddenly shook itself free of the lighting wires.

As, complete with ticket machine and cash bag, she hung on for dear life, shouting blue murder to "get me doon!", the driver, torn between seeing if he'd killed anyone in the flat and getting his clippie back to earth, panicked, and it wasn't until the crew of a following 107 arrived on scene a few minutes later, that willing hands managed to bring the clippie back to earth. If only I had had my camera with me in the days when mobile phones hadn't been invented. You just don't get drama like that with a diesel bus!

A couple of days later, the overhead line department had strung a protective mesh of wires from the end of the bridge to the next traction pole, as it turned out it wasn't the first time that this good lady had experienced the trauma of a trolleyhead through her kitchen window. Joe Doherty told me that the clippie fully recovered, despite her airborne trauma, while the department paid for a new window, retrieved the trolleyhead and, after a thorough investigation, awarded the driver a two-day suspension, for, as Joe Doherty said, he was well-known for having dewirements.

The crews themselves would add to the street theatre, for at Hampden Garage there was a great variety of people in the cab and on the platform. Some were long-service staff who had transferred from the trams. They were sticklers for the rule book, wore their uniforms with pride and lived the job as real Trolleybus People.

Others were from Donegal and the Punjab, while there were, of course, plenty of native Glaswegians, and, by the time the system closed, some staff joined for a few years or even months only, and left for other jobs. Many of the Pakistanis stayed for a few years and used the money earned to buy corner shops, while others went into

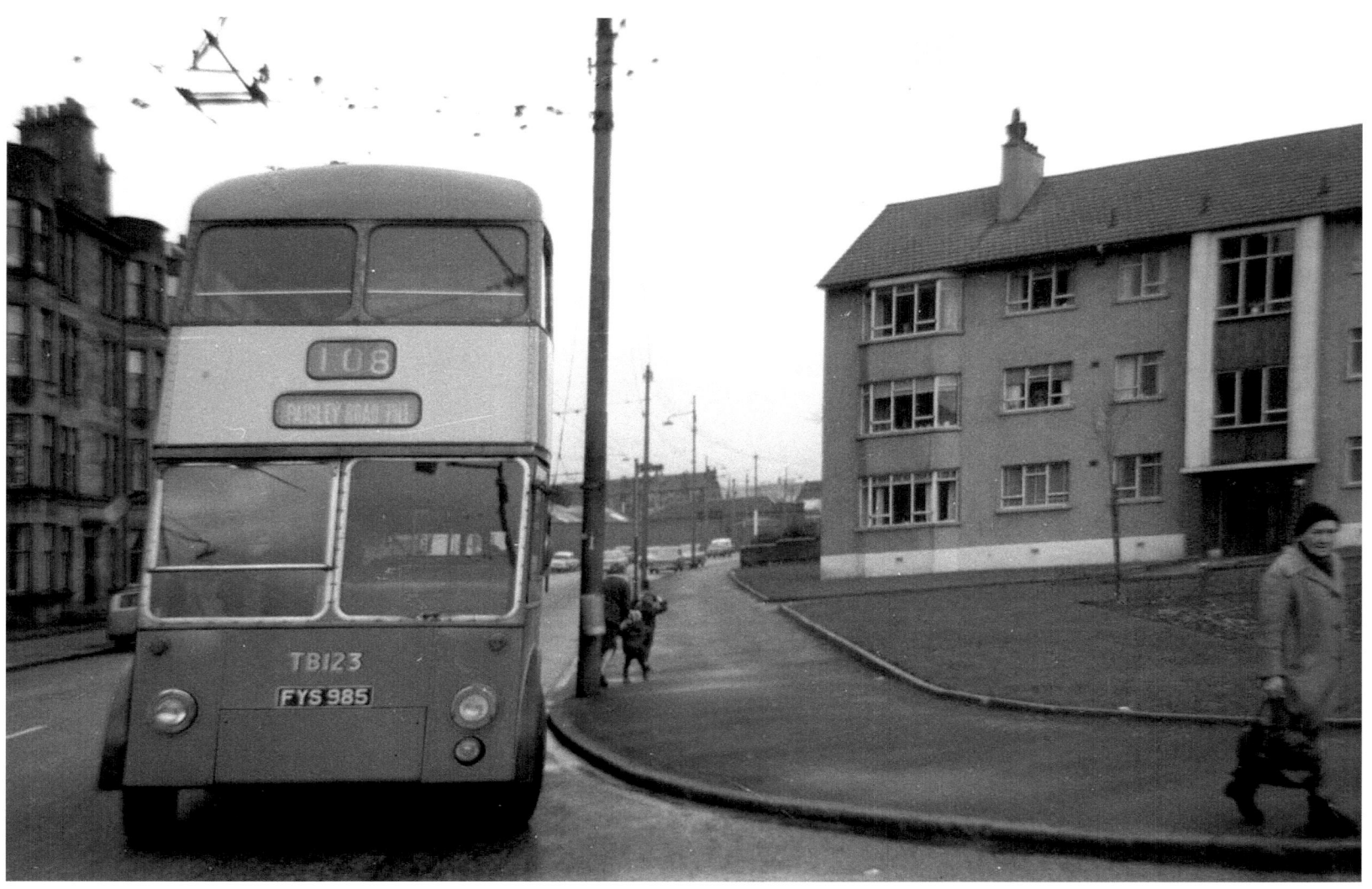
How not to change the frogs! TB123 turns onto the turning curve built specially for the trolleys heading for Mount Florida Terminus at Ballogie Road. Look carefully and you'll see her frog pole stuck in the pull wire hook, as she struggles to untangle it. March 1966. *Hugh Dougherty*

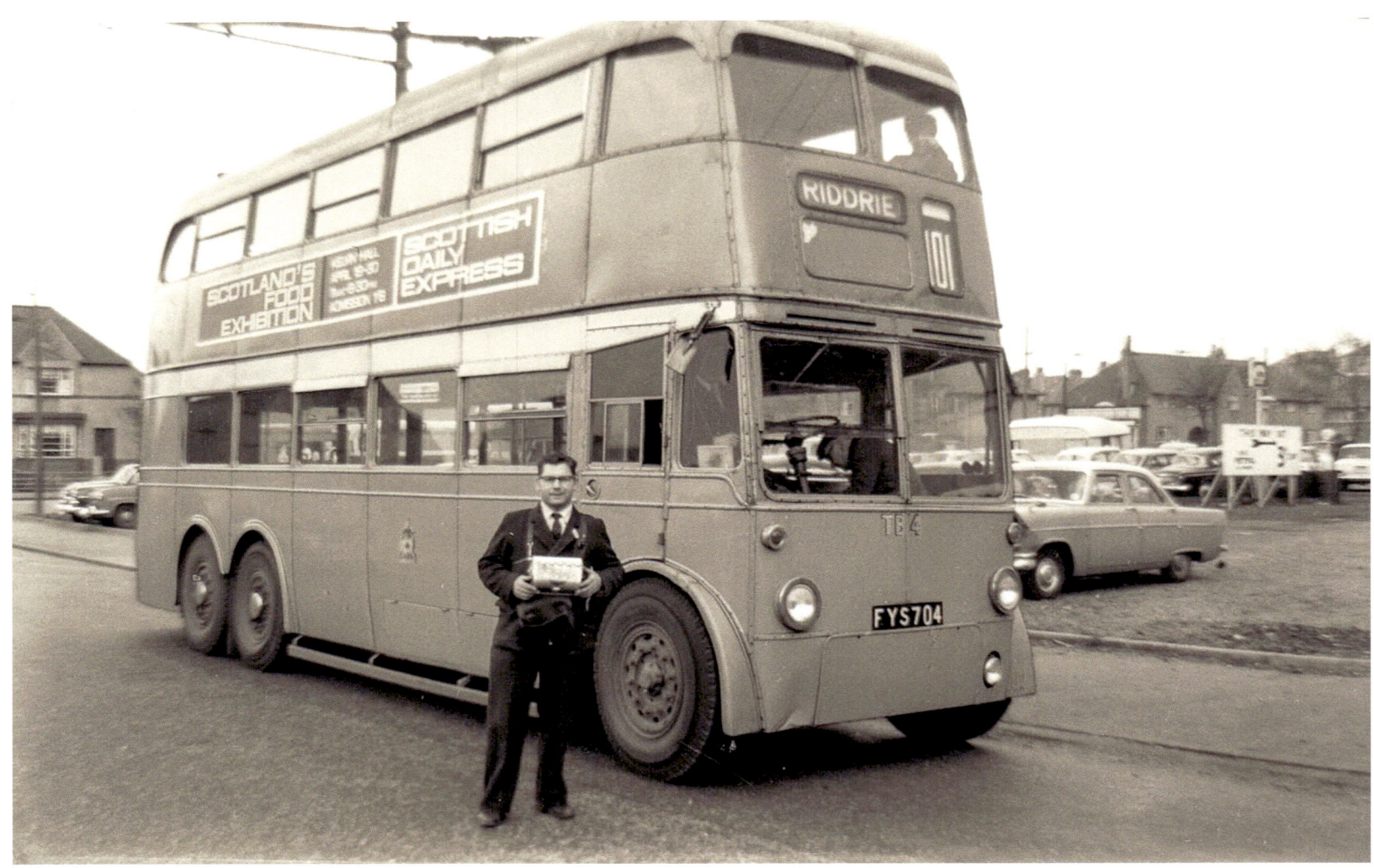

Conductors and clippies played a key role in the street theatre of the trolleys. Conductor Archie Bertram, with his Ultimate tickets machine and leather cash bag worn in the regulation way, poses in front of TB4 at Rutherglen Terminus on 29th April 1966, while a wee boy looks on from the top deck. A fitter is in the cab beside the driver, who has the time board beside him, fixing a sticking contactor. *Hugh Dougherty*

professions either here or back at home. Many Donegal folk stayed, too, and made a career on the trolleys, but, again, others went home.

I can remember one Pakistani conductor asking me which way was East at Muirend, so he could direct his prayers in the right direction, and the Sikh and Pakistani Muslim staff, who had made huge adjustments on coming to Glasgow to work on the trolleys, were invariably good at their job and polite. The same could not always be said, sadly, of some of the Glaswegian drifters who came into the job in later days, wearing their uniforms slovenly, breaking the rules and giving the inspectors, upholders of standards, nightmares.

The Trolleybus Section rule book stipulated: "Conductors should announce clearly the name of the next stopping place in good time to inform passengers wishing to alight." By the mid-sixties, this had largely died out, but one elderly conductor, dressed in a tram driver's motorman's coat – he had transferred to the trolleys rather than surrender to the dreaded diesels when Langside Tram Depot closed – wore his cap like a guardsman, and his ticket machine and cash bag in the regulation way. With his machine square on the chest and the cash bag flap secured under, he would call all the fare stages on the 105 and 107.

That included "Gorbals Cross where I was born!" "Queen's Park Gates for a walk in the park!" and "Battlefield Rest for the Victoria Infirmary!" He also had his passengers categorised, addressing women travelling south as far as Govanhill 'hen', 'missus' between there and Cathcart railway bridge, and 'madam', from there onwards towards Muirend and over the Renfrewshire boundary to Clarkston.

Clippies tended to be the best for banter, such as replying to questions, such as: "Do youse go to the dancin'?" the reply being, "Naw, and ma' trolley doesna'e dance either. But we do pass the Palais, hen." Clippies would often bring a tranny along with them, a tranny, then, being a transistor radio, and listen to it at the terminus, while telling passengers off for breaking the silence of the trolleybus while en route by playing a tranny to the annoyance of other passengers.

Platform staff were also good at dealing with the inevitable Glasgow drunks swarming on board after pub, evening, closing time at 10 past 10. Some were happy, some sang, and some kept quiet, but the occasional one was up for a fight, so much so that there was concern about behaviour on the trolleys.

In 1964 police patrolled the 101 and 102s on Royston Road, with several arrests, one after a chase by police using a trolleybus to catch up with the one on front, on which two drunk men were shouting and swearing while standing on the back platform. The magistrate at Glasgow Central Police Court, fining a 48 year-old woman £20, who had been shouting and swearing on a 106 trolleybus in Bridgeton's Abercrombie Street, and who admitted to three previous convictions for similar, trolleybus-borne, offences told her: "Don't you read the papers? Don't you know about the trouble there has been on the buses?"

In 1964, my father, a fanatical Celtic supporter, as were all the Glasgow Irish Catholic teachers of his generation, decided to leave his car at home and take the 105 from Mount Florida to Queen's Cross, as the terminus was right outside Partick Thistle's ground where Celtic was playing Thistle. I went with him, and unusually, we went upstairs, which suited me fine to view the route and the passing trolleys, which, to be frank, interested me more than Celtic.

All was well until we hit the Glasssford Street/Argyle Street stop, and the otherwise lightly-loaded trolley was invaded by a horde of baying Schelic fans. In those days, before football merchandising, no one wore team jerseys, just scarves scarves and the odd Celtic bunnet. Wee men, and there were lots of wee men in Glasgow in those days, wore cloth caps and raincoats, and, as the trolley picked up speed, the one behind us, opened his coat to reveal a set of pockets, one of which held a bottle of Lanliq, better known as 'Lanny', a popular cheap wine of the day, and, incredibly, a set of glasses. He selected one, poured out his Lanny and proceeded to drink it as we went along up West Nile Street, tapping my douce Dad on the shoulder to ask: "Do ye want a swally, ma friend?" My Dad politely declined.

Meanwhile, the clippie, a large lady, with her ticket machine worn well forward, her departmental forage cap perched atop a superbly-crafted beehive hairdo, in light-up-the-night blonde, immaculate uniform, clearly a clippie who took no prisoners, came upstairs, bellowing, with great authority: "Ferrs puleese!"

Most fans paid up, but in front of us there were two, who, unusually for the time, had conversed with a liberal peppering of 'fs' and 'cs', until my father, ready to explode, had addressed them in best teacher's voice and told them to desist.

Incredibly, they did, but when the clippie asked for their fares, they invited her to "f off! We're Shelic fans and we're no payin'!" "Aye ye ur!" she shouted back and gave the bell push several dings. With the driver's immediate application of the rheostatic and air brakes, very sharp when applied as in this emergency, the trolley stood on its nose, and in what seemed seconds, there was a very large, Donegal driver standing beside the clippie. He was carrying the frog changing pole.

"Youse are off, if ye's don't pay!" he bellowed, pointing at the miscreants with his pole. That was enough. They meekly tendered their fares and the clippie smashed the tickets down on their palms to let show who was in charge. Our journey continued on a very quiet and orderly 105. That was how a crisis was dealt with in the days before radios and mobile phones. It was a simpler world.

But, Glasgow gangs were also to the fore, and crews had to deal with Cumbie neds on routes through the Gorbals, the Maryhill Fleet around Queen's Cross, and the Govan Team on the 106, to name but a few. Trolleys began to be vandalised internally. When TB78's upper deck was being prepared for repainting at Sandtoft Trolleybus Museum, the late Brian Deans, doyen of Glasgow trolleybus enthusiasts, and author of *Glasgow Trolleybuses*, the definitive work on the system, told me that he found the battle cry: "Cumbie ya bass!" scratched into the paintwork, showing that the trolley must indeed have run the gantlet in Gorbals!

Conducting was hard work, for, apart from tokens given by some employers to staff to pay their fares on work journeys, all else was in cash, in those pre-decimal days, using combinations of large and heavy pennies, thruppenny bits, as Glaswegians called them, sixpences, shillings, florins and half-crowns.

If a clippie or conductor received a note, usually a ten bob, that is, ten shilling, note, known as half a dollar in Glasgow, and, very occasionally, a pound note, they would deftly swing open the front of their Ultimate ticket machine, and lodge the note behind the ticket roll chamber, firmly clipping the machine back together to keep the notes secure.

The black, leather cash bags, many of which carried a "Glasgow Corporation Tramways", embossed buckle, weighed heavily on the shoulder at the end of a busy shift as many people would use the trolley for one or two stops on streets with shopping habits radically different from today. Following rush hours, when passengers heading into town, would, in 1966, pay one shilling for a journey of over six stages, from Clarkston on the 105 to Cowcaddens, or, later in the morning, 4d for two stages, from Battlefield to the then-fashionable Victoria Road and its shops, on the 107, conductors and clippies were kept very busy.

You would still get wee women with bag washes going to the steamie, the municipal wash house, with the bag left under the stairs between stops. As most people shopped daily for fresh food such as butcher meat, bread, fish and milk, there were plenty of local shops all along the route serving their communities. Shops, on hot days, extended their canopies over their windows, and staff would serve customers, just as the conductor served them on the trolleybus. It was so different from our self-service world, although, by the end of the system in 1967, supermarkets were making their appearance, one of the first being at Muirend, close to where trolleybus crews stamped their Bundy cards.

Conducting was a busy job which kept people fit, constantly running up and down the stair to collect fares, belling the driver, stamping the Bundy card, changing the frogs, issuing the right value tickets, giving the right change, regulating the number of passengers on the trolleybus, writing up the waybill and transfer slips, changing the destination blind, and helping deal with dewirements, while keeping good order and looking after passengers who needed a hand. After all that, they had to cash in the correct amount at the end of the shift.

It was no sinecure and neither was the job of the man in the cab who had to deal with increasing traffic during the lifespan on the trolleybuses from 1949 to 1967, making sure that the bus safely negotiated frogs, section gaps and crossings on the overhead wires, and above, all, running to time. To run late or, worse still, in the eyes of the Corporation, early, or out of order with another trolley where routes met, such as the 105 and 107, or the 101 and 102, and failing to follow the timeboard which every trolleybus carried in service, was to incur the wrath of inspectors.

Known to the green staff as 'The Gestapo', they wore superior quality uniforms and, many having served in the forces during the

RULES FOR CONDUCTORS

134. Position on trolleybus.—The Conductor's post when on duty, and not engaged in collecting fares, is on the rear platform. He should stand facing the road, ready to attend to passengers and on the alert for intending passengers. He must not sit down in the trolleybus, nor engage his attention by reading, talking to passengers or employees, nor should he do anything which will interfere with the prompt and efficient performance of his duties. Should he need to consult his Driver, he should do so while the trolleybus is halted at a stopping-place. In an emergency he may signal the Driver to stop the trolleybus and he may then go round the front of the trolleybus. Bulkhead window must be kept closed, Conductor must not talk to the Driver through this window or interfere with him in any way while he is operating his trolleybus.

135. Trolley Booms.—Before putting booms on wires Conductor must ensure that trolley heads swivel freely, when putting booms on overhead wires they also must ensure that booms are swivelling freely at trolley base. The metal ring must be used when pulling booms down from wires.

136. Manually operated frog.—When trolleybus is turning at manually operated frog, Conductor will change frog with pole. He will make sure that the indicator light is showing for the direction the trolleybus is going.

137. Unfamiliar or excessive noise.—Conductor must inform his Driver immediately if he hears any unfamiliar or excessive noise coming from trolley heads or overhead wires or from any other part of the vehicle.

138. Stand by trolleybuses.—Conductors must stand by trolleybuses during the temporary absence of Drivers.

139. Running in to garage.—When trolleybus is running into garage, Conductor must close all windows and must remain on trolleybus until it is parked.

140. Leaving duty.—Should a Conductor be unable to complete his duty through sickness or other such emergency, he should hand over ticket machine, waybills, tickets, box, and other articles to any official or employee of the Department having authority to receive same. He shall be responsible in such a case, for paying in the cash he has collected to the Garage Office.

141. Naming Stations.—Conductors should announce clearly the name of the next stopping place in good time to inform passengers wishing to alight.

142. Stopping places.—Conductors should commit to memory the names of stopping-places on the routes upon which they operate, they should keep a **sharp look-out** at all stopping-places and **at termini,** for intending passengers, at all stopping-places, passengers must be allowed reasonable time to board or alight. While a trolleybus is not carrying its full complement of passengers, stops must be made even if the trolleybus is behind scheduled time. If the trolleybus is full, or disabled, the Conductor should, where possible, give this information to persons waiting at stopping place.

143. Responsibility for equipment.—Conductors will be held responsible for padlock and key, ticket machine, or punch, and ticket box, and all other articles under their charge.

Conductors had to be on their toes, as these two pages of the Rule Book require.

Hugh Dougherty

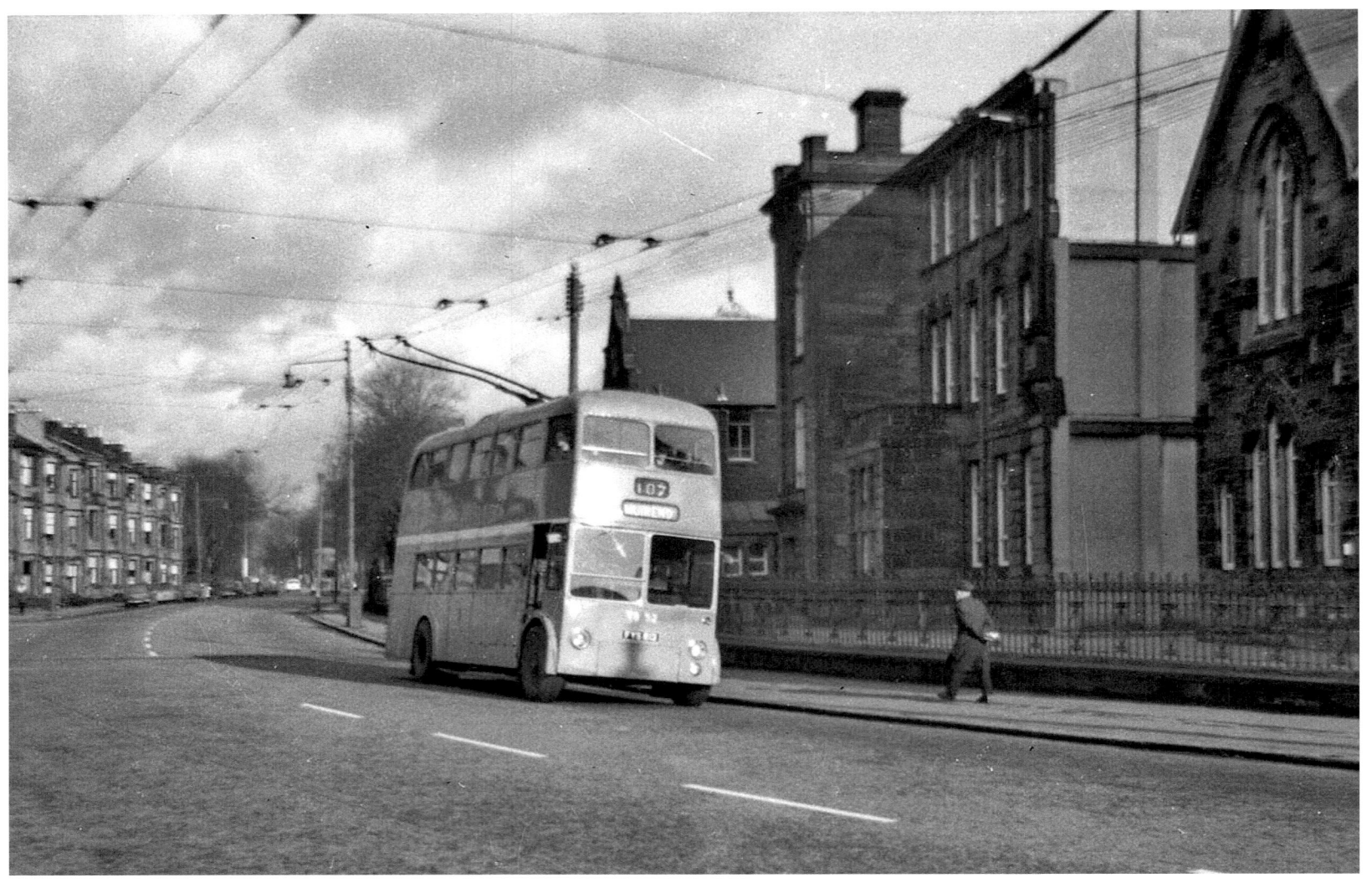

Beware trolley drivers who ran early! A member of the Gestapo, having emerged from his bunker within Battlefield Rest, heads toward TB52 on the 107, to grill the driver. The old Queen's Park Secondary School provides the backdrop in February 1967. *Hugh Dougherty*

Second World War, were sticklers for discipline. Most wore Glasgow Corporation Transport long service badges and many were quite scary. Some checked tickets, seizing the conductor's waybill on boarding, and going round the trolley to check every ticket. A missed fare, a wrongly-issued ticket or an incorrect fare stage printed on a ticket could all result in a booking.

Others lurked in their 'Gestapo bunkers', as in the ornate and former tram shelter of Battlefield Rest, or, at Bridgeton Cross, from which they would emerge from their wee, green hut, to check the passing time of trolleys, and woe betide any driver failing to meet their exacting standards. Battlefield Rest, now a popular Italian Restaurant, displayed, until it was closed as a bus shelter by Greater Glasgow Passenger Transport Executive in the 1970s, a mural of a lady in period dress hailing a Glasgow motorbus of the early 1930s. "Always Signal from the Kerb", was its exhortation, a reference to the fact that Glaswegians, used to walking out into the middle of the road to board trams, did the same with the first motorbuses, and, later, the trolleybuses, with some fatal results. The 'silent death' tag attached to the Glasgow trolleybus, seems to have its origin in the phenomenon of walking out into the road, the trolley being deemed more lethal as you would hear a diesel bus coming, and you certainly knew when a tram was on its way.

Other street theatre came from trolleys sparking on the overhead wires and they did this quite spectacularly on cold, icy mornings. Although a trolleybus, fitted with special, metal trolleyheads, to break the overnight ice film, toured the system before regular service started, I can well remember waiting for my 107 on cold mornings and watching spectacular displays of sparks as a trolley passed in the other direction. On foggy days, and there were plenty then, the displays were even better, with the flashes seemingly detached from the bus below.

After dark trolleys would light up the sky as the booms passed below section gaps and frogs. A family friend, who grew up in the heart of the Irish community in a tenement at Gorbals Cross, where the 107 and 105 crossed the 106, remembers lying in bed at night and watching the ceiling being lit up as the trolleys passed the building.

"It was quite spectacular," she recalled, "and very much part of life at Gorbals Cross which still had tenements, shops, plenty of people, pubs in every corner, a clock on the centre trolleybus pole and a gents public toilet on the island in the centre of the cross, and, of course, trolleybuses passing every few minutes."

Part of the reason why she saw such displays was that drivers were less likely after dark to obey the rule book instruction to take their feet off the power pedal when passing under a dead section, and to notch up again carefully after, as there were fewer inspectors around, and runs into the garage were usually taken quickly.

Occasionally, the overhead wires would break. If the trolley wires, the two from which the trolley booms took their current, did this, as opposed to the span wires which, attached to buildings and traction poles, held them up, the driver had to don a pair of heavy-duty rubber gloves, carried in the cab. He then had to grasp the

Conductor John Dolan was on the 105 on the last day of service on 27th May 1967, handing over his trolley to a relieving crew.   *Hugh Dougherty*

TB 104	Cowcaddens	Homlea Rd	15/5/67	6a
TB 73	Homlea Rd	Cowcaddens	16/5/67	6a
TB 76	Cowcaddens	Homlea Rd	16/5/67	6
TB 116	King's Park Rd	Cowcaddens	17/5/67	6
TB 113	Cowcaddens	Homlea Rd	17/5/67	6
TB 78	Homlea Rd	Cowcaddens	18/5/67	6
TB 78	Cowcaddens	Homlea Rd	18/5/67	6
TB 106	Homlea Rd	Cowcaddens	19/5/67	6
TB 117	George Sq	Homlea Rd	19/5/67	6
TB 107	Homlea Rd	Queens Cross	20/5/67	1/-
TB 107	Queen's Cross	Homlea Rd	20/5/67	1/-
TB 75	King's Park	Cowcaddens	22/5/67	6
TB 73	Cowcaddens	George Square	22/5/67	6
TB 124	Cowcaddens	Mount Florida	22/5/67	6
TB 78	Homlea Rd	Cowcaddens	23/5/67	6
TB 65	Cowcaddens	Homlea Rd	23/5/67	6
TB 73	Homlea Rd	Clarkston	23/5/67	1/-
TB 73	Clarkston	Queens X	23/5/67	1/-
TB 104	Queens X	Mount Florida	23/5/67	1/-
TB 106	King's Park Rd	Cowcaddens	24/5/67	6
TB 102	Cowcaddens	Homlea Rd	24/5/67	6
TB 106	Homlea Rd	Clarkston	25/5/67	8
TB 106	Clarkston	Homlea Rd	25/5/67	8a
TB 73	Homlea Rd	Cowcaddens	26/5/67	6a
	Last run to school by Trolleybus ✪			
TB 69	George Sq	Cowcaddens	26/5/67	6a
TB 103	Maitland St	Mount Florida	26/5/67	10c
	Last Run Home by Trolleybus			
TB 66	Homlea Rd	Clarkston	26/5/67	8a
TB 66	Clarkston	King's Park Rd	26/5/67	★
TB 123	Last Run Queens X – Clarkston		27/5/67	10w

★ Last Run by Normal Service Trolleybus.

✪ Ticket issued on TB 73 on Last Run by Trolleybus to School.

Last Ticket to be issued by Trolleybus from Maitland St

Pages from my wee green book, showing the sort of information I recorded nearly 60 years ago. It was another world.

Hugh Dougherty

107

Date	T/Bus No	Time at Maitland
26/2/67	TB 96	3.55 a.m.
George Square	4·00 p.m.	TB 37 TB 53 TB 120
Trongate	4·02 p.m.	TB 70 TB 78 TB
Gorbals Cross	4·06 p.m.	TB 116 TB 117 TB
Eglinton Toll	4·10 p.m.	TB 121 TB 47 TB
Q.P. Gates	4·13 p.m.	TB 110 TB 112 TB

Date	T/Bus No	Time at Battlefield
23/2/67	TB 100	8.86 a.m.
Eglinton Toll	8·12 am	TB 46 TB 38
Gorbals Cross	8·15 am	TB 113 TB 69
Trongate	8·17 am	TB 721 TB 110
Geo. P. Sq.	8·21 am	TB 47 TB
Maitland St	8·25 am	TB 102 TB

Date	T/Bus No	Time at Maitland St
27/2/67	TB 121	4·11 p.m.
George Sq	4·16 p.m.	TB 124 TB 55 TB
Trongate	4·19 p.m.	TB 38 TB 26 TB
Gorbals Cross	4·24 p.m.	TB 76 TB 102 TB
Eglinton Toll	4·27 p.m.	TB 124 TB 49 TB
Q.P. Gates	4·30 p.m.	TB 67 TB 91 TB

107

Date	T/Bus No	Time at Battlefield
23/2/67	TB 120	8.5
Eglinton Toll	8·10	Passed
Gorbals Cross	8·13	TB 46
Trongate	8·17	TB 62
George Sq.	8·19	TB 121
Maitland St	8·24	

Date	T/Bus No	Time at M.S. Battlefield
23/2/67	TB 121	4·17 h
George Sq.	4·18	TB 100 TB 62
Trongate	4·20	TB 113 TB 75
Gorbals Cross	4·22	TB 46 TB 70
Eglinton Toll	4·25	TB 109
Q.P. Gates	4·29	TB 78

Date	T/Bus No	Time at Battlefield
24/2/67	TB 70	8·12 am
Eglinton Toll	8·17 am	TB 121 TB 120
Gorbals Cross	8·22 am	TB 62 TB 75
Trongate	8·26 am	TB 76 TB
George Sq.	8·28 am	TB 102 TB
Maitland St	8·31 am	TB 74 TB

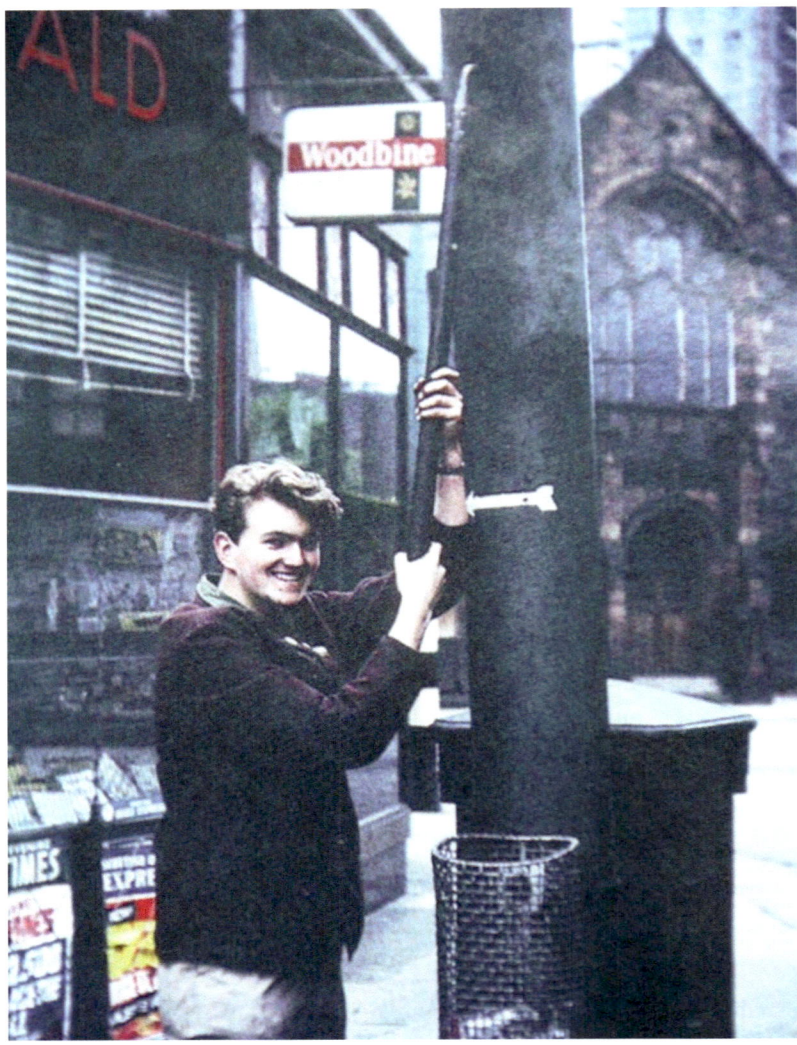

Hugh changes the frogs at King's Park Road with his frog pole on the last trolleybus tour on Saturday 27th May 1967. *The late Brian Deans*

wires, which the rule book reminded him, carried 600 volts DC, and pull them out of the way of traffic, brave man that he was. What would today's health and safety culture make of that?

I would often see the overhead line department's maroon tower wagons fixing faults in frogs and other wiring defects. The remarkable thing about these highly-skilled men, all of whom had worked on tramway overhead as well as trolleybuses equipment, seemed to wear the same garb, come rain or shine, consisting of a cloth bunnet and an ancient sports jacket over a set of overalls or dungarees. They must have been waterproofed at birth, or that workwear, as we understand it today, hadn't been invented.

For they hadn't hard hats, waterproof or reflective jackets, and the gangs worked on their tower wagon platforms with the power on, being protected from electric shock if and when they had to touch both positive and negative trolley wires, thanks to rubber-soled boots and their wagon's insulated platform. They attracted public attention and added to the street theatre below by signalling passing trolleybuses to drop their booms and pass the tower wagon on battery power, before connecting up again to the overhead.

The mysteries of overhead line men who didn't get electrocuted were explained to me when I visited the overhead line department, which was based in what were the horse tram stables at Coplawhill Car Works. There, a few weeks before the end of the trolleys, I met the boss, the gentlemanly Mr Lawn, who presided over his crews, all dedicated to their craft and saddened greatly by the impending end of the system.

I was shown overhead line equipment close up, and it was massive and heavy, when not seen from pavement level. I was taught everything there was to learn about insulators, pull off wires, curved segments, section insulators and electrically-operated frogs which were worked by the driver. Passing under a skate in the overhead, whose position was marked by a silver stud in the road, the driver glided under it to go straight on, and struck one notch of power to access the diverging wires. Glasgow removed the last of these before the closure as it was felt that the arrangement led to dewirements, and so, it was back to handpoles.

I was also shown an original set of insulators from the first Glasgow electric tram route of 1898, and was sent home with a

The all-important time board whose figures had to be adhered to at all times. If a dewirement, such as the incident of the flying trolley head at Cathcart railway bridge held up a trolley, much report writing was required.

Hugh Dougherty

souvenir of a short length of cadmium copper trolley wire, so strong that you simply can't bend it, with an ear, the clamp that fits into a groove on it, to allow the trolley to run underneath, while the ear screws on to an insulator. It sits beside me as I write this, a mute tribute to skills lost in time and men who worked aloft with dedication and pride, to keep the trolleys running.

After the last trolleybus ran, Mr Lawn and his men had the depressing task of cutting down the wires they had worked hard to keep in tip top condition, and you would see them on their platforms, severing the trolley wires at each set of hangers, before cutting down the span wires. The wires went for scrap, although some did make it to Sandtoft Trolleybus Museum in Doncaster and to Crich Tramway Village in Derbyshire, where they form part of the working overhead at each operating museum. All the overhead line staff retired or were made redundant, although some were snapped up by British Railways to work on their Blue Train overhead wires, where their expertise was both valued and welcomed.

TROLLEYBUS SERVICE No. 105

With effect from SUNDAY, 28th MAY, 1967, Trolleybus Service No. 105 will be *Replaced* by Motorbus Service No. 66, which will operate between Clarkston or Muirend and Queen's Cross via the same route. There will be some alterations to the timetable, details of which may be obtained from 46 Bath Street, Glasgow, C.2.

46 BATH STREET
GLASGOW, C.2

CORPORATION  TRANSPORT

E. R. L. FITZPAYNE
General Manager

Notice of the end of the 105 service Glasgow's last trolleybus route and its replacement.

Lewis Hutton collection

When the system closed, most trolleybus crews transferred to motor buses at Larkfield and Langside Garages, but, for drivers, that meant retraining on diesels and sitting a Public Service Vehicle test, as a trolleybus driver, legally, a trackless tram driver, sat a Ministry of Transport trolleybus only test, and was not qualified to drive diesels.

That meant learning how to use gears, as trolleybus speed was governed by the power pedal only, as well as having to forget about having overhead wires, and many retrained drivers said that they missed the smoothness of the trolleybus. Above all, former trolleybus drivers had to adapt to the accelerator and brake being the other way round on the diesels, something that some found hard to master, and, I well remember going to school in 1968, a year after the trolleys were killed off, on a front entrance Leyland Atlantean, which was involved in a smash.

I boarded the bus on the 67, the replacement for the 107, and recognised the driver, a younger man who had driven at Hampden. We exchanged a friendly nod, and I went upstairs. As we passed Eglinton Toll, doing about 20mph, a van darted out of a side street, right in front of the bus, and instead of braking we accelerated, going right into the van's side.

On the way down the stairs, where the driver was still sitting, shocked, at the wheel, with the whole dash panel lying on the road, he was saying to his equally-shocked conductor: "I thought I was braking." His trolleybus instinct had taken over and he'd automatically pressed what his brain told him was the brake. I gave the conductor my name and address as a witness as the van driver was clearly at fault, but there were other near misses, Joe Doherty told me, for exactly the same reason, when electric drivers were forced to adapt to internal combustion.

On the night of the last trolleybus into Hampden Garage on Saturday 27th May 1967, the final drama of the Glasgow trolleybuses was enacted with the crews lingering to sing 'We're no awa tae bide awa', as they headed into the dark to face a new future at Larkfield and Langside, while Glasgow Corporation had pulled the plug on electric street traction after 69 years of service to the city by tram and trolleybus.

I was there as a passenger on the Scottish Tramway Museum Society Last Trolleybus Tour to witness the funeral, and, although just 16, I was struck by a profound sense of sadness and a feeling that Glasgow had lost something worthwhile under the guise of imagined progress.

Today, you can still see trolleybus relics, such as Muirend turning circle, the trolleybuses slip road between King's Park and Carmunnock Roads, the last trolleybus silver stud indicator to drivers at Ballogie Road's Mount Florida Terminus, and the odd traction pole that once held up the trolleybus wires. TBS 13, one of the single deckers that once graced the 108 route, is in Riverside Museum and TB78, the only working Glasgow trolleybus left, runs at Sandtoft Trolleybus Museum, but it's a tragedy that the city's faithful, and environmentally-friendly silent service was scrapped with such haste, nearly six decades ago.

I've ridden on modern trolleybuses since, in cities such as Vancouver or Salzburg, which have embraced and developed their systems and are continuing to do so. If Glasgow had also kept its trolleys, the city would now be in the forefront of providing green and attractive public transport. Battery buses, with their teething problems and inefficient, heavy batteries, are no substitute for Glasgow's trolleybuses that were squandered in 1967. Time, then, to bring them back, now that a silent service is seen as a virtue in itself?

Last Trolleybus ticket issued on the tour run by the Scottish Tramway Museum Society on 27th May 1967.

Hugh Dougherty

45

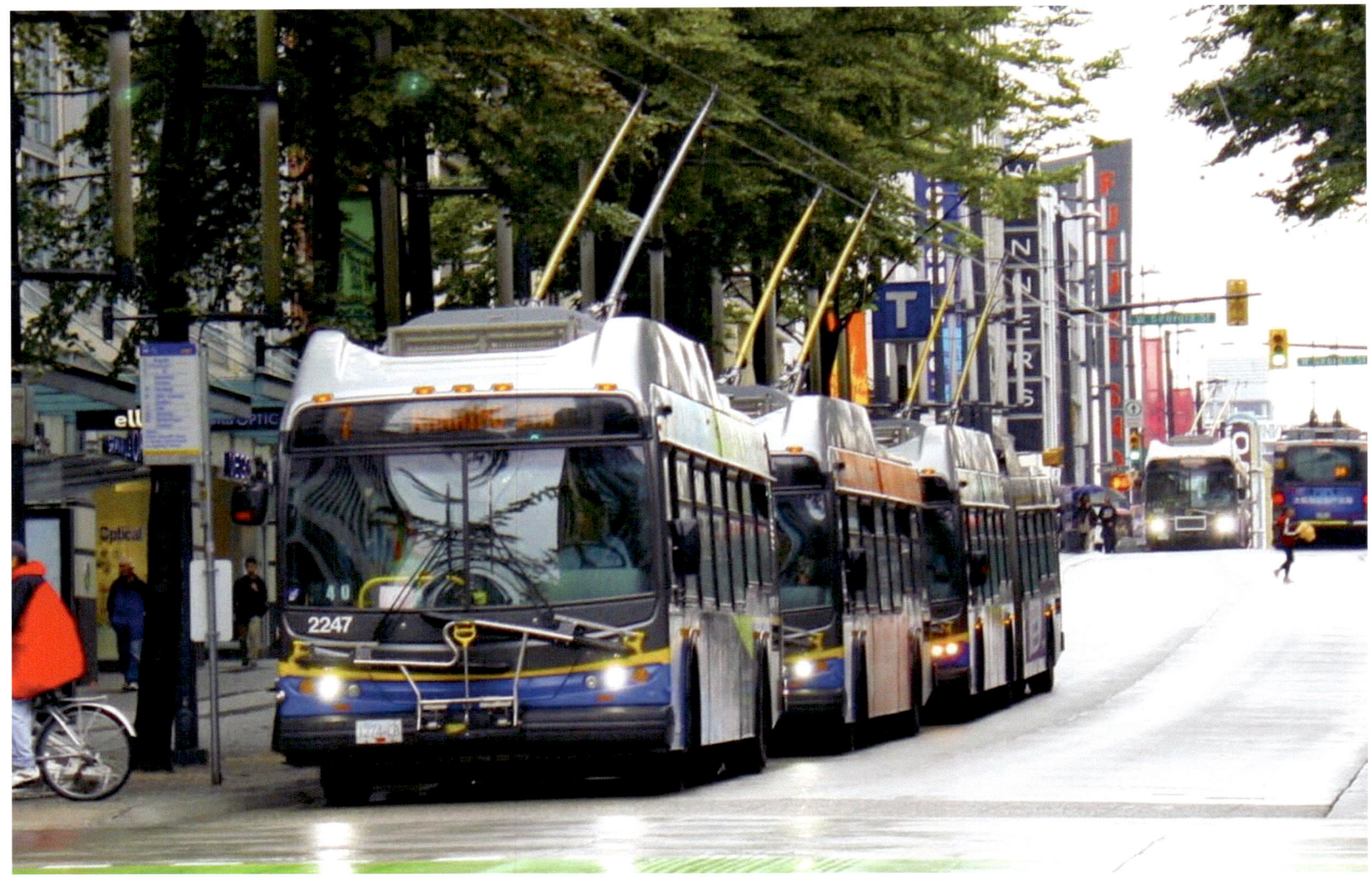

Trolleybus-only Granville Street in Vancouver. Vancouver opened its first trolleybus route in 1948, one year before Glasgow, and has developed and expanded its system. This is what we could have today in Glasgow. *Hugh Dougherty*

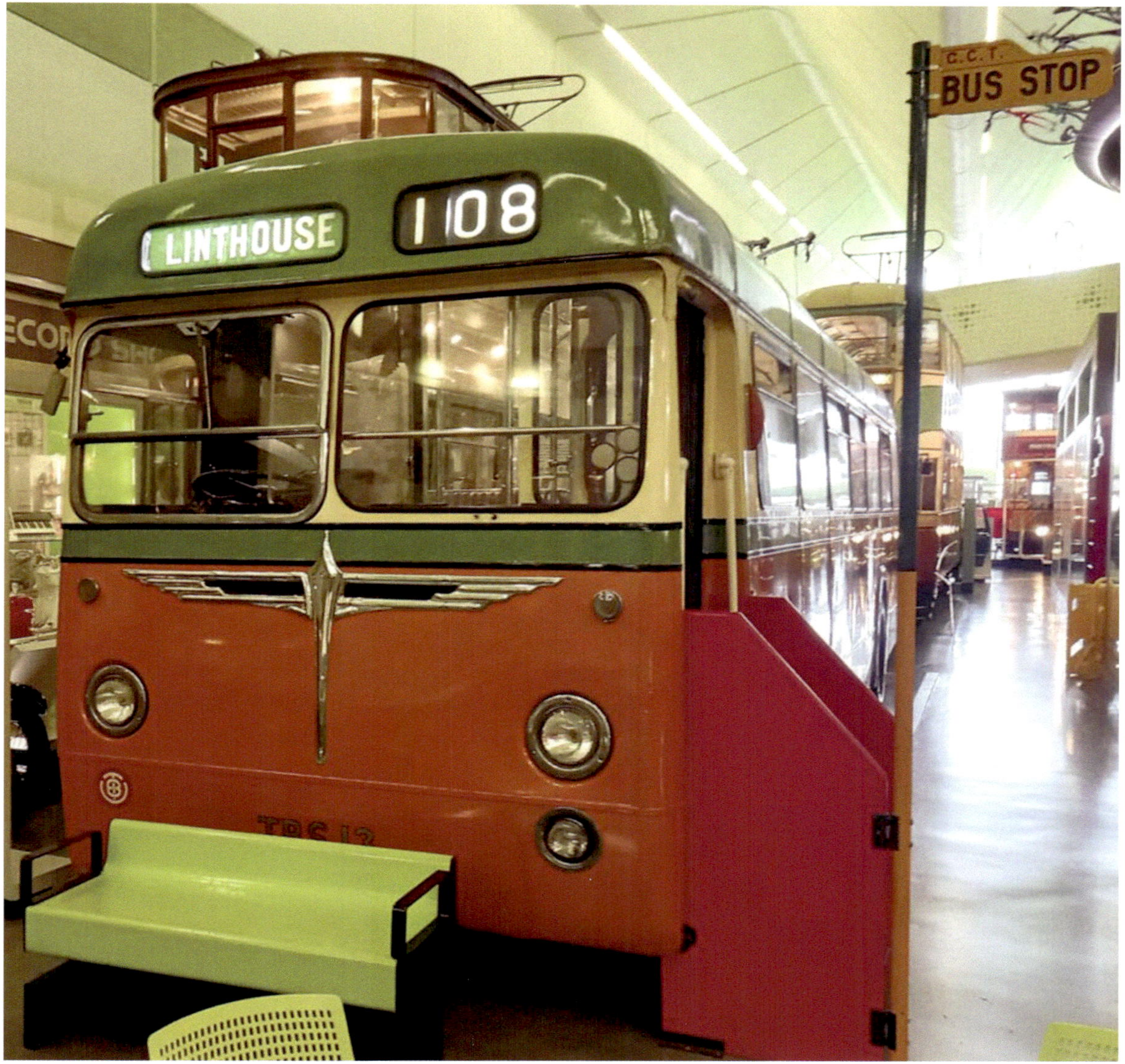

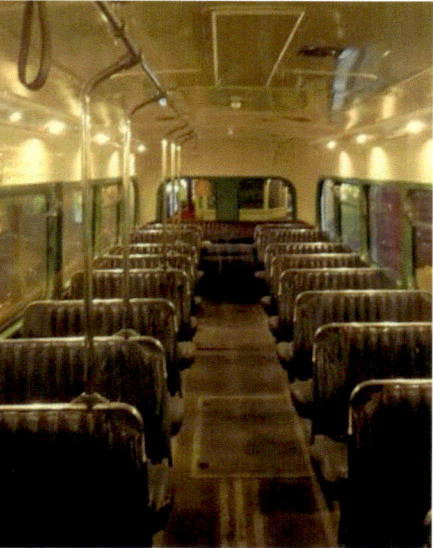

TBS 13 has survived at Glasgow's Riverside Museum as a reminder of Glasgow's brief encounter with trolleybuses.

Hugh Dougherty

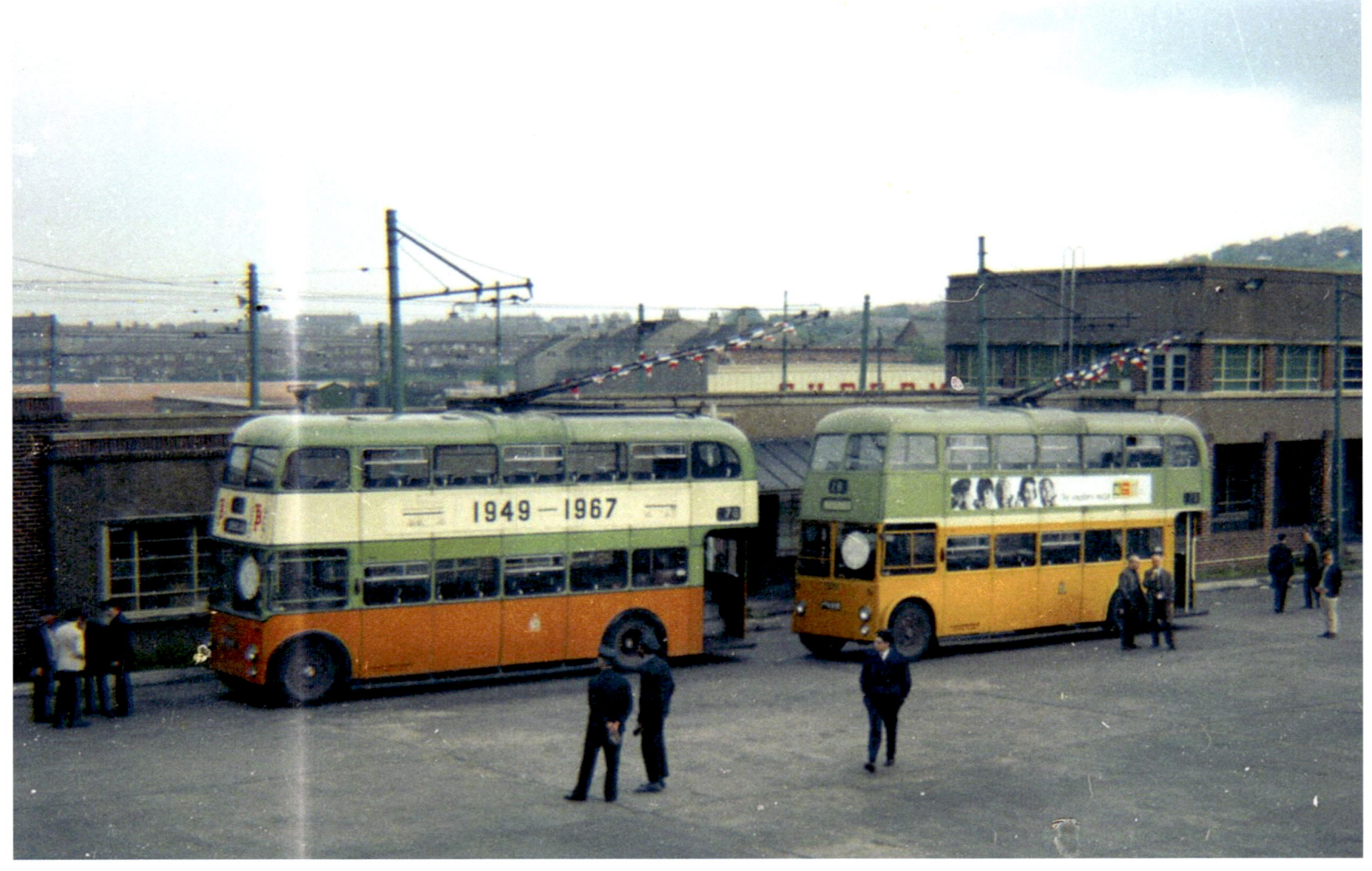

The sad scene as the last trolleybus tour gets ready to set off from Hampden on Saturday 27th May 1967, with TB123 and TB78 taking up duty. TB78 survives today in running order at Sandtoft Trolleybus Museum near Doncaster. *Hugh Dougherty*